TREASURES FOUND:
Devotion

Dell Anne Hines Afzal

WESTBOW
PRESS
A DIVISION OF THOMAS NELSON

WestBow Press books may be ordered through booksellers or by contacting:

WestBow Press
A Division of Thomas Nelson
1663 Liberty Drive
Bloomington, IN 47403
www.westbowpress.com
1-(866) 928-1240

Author photo taken by Shaida Afzal Ehlert.

ISBN: 978-1-4497-9546-7 (sc)
ISBN: 978-1-4497-9547-4 (hc)
ISBN: 978-1-4497-9545-0 (e)

Library of Congress Control Number: 2013909007

Printed in the United States of America.

WestBow Press rev. date: 5/21/2013

ACKNOWLEDGMENT

This publication of my family history is dedicated to my mother, Lois Marion and to the memory of my late father, Charles Henry Hines with much love, adoration and thanks for my safety, life lessons, humor and memories.

The words are my own and are written in tribute to two people who have meant the world to me my entire life. My thanks go to my mother for her patience in my early years and now here in my later years for listening to my fears and short-comings, for they are many.

I wish to thank my husband, Naser and my children for their shoulders and strength when I cried while reliving the past. This has been a tremendously cleansing journey.

I also wish to thank my first cousin, Robert D. Smith, owner of First Image in Franklin, Tennessee AKA *TheRobertD* and author of *20,000 Days and Counting* published by *Thomas Nelson*.

Even though you arrived in my world five and a half years later than I, your inspiration has forced me to open my mouth to allow my words to fall. Your teachings have allowed me to find a voice in my later years and relate stories of our family for those who follow.

I thank you, *TheRobertD* from the bottom of my heart. I hope my words reflect your inspiration and how you continue to impact me and my thinking.

Dell Anne Hines Afzal

Author, Dell Anne Hines Afzal and *TheRobertD*,
Robert D. Smith together again

CONTENTS

PROLOGUE – Treasures Found

From his favorite spot on the breezeway with a mischievous grin on his face he greeted two of his four 'cubs' Dell Anne and Nola Jane. Following close behind was Nola Jane's husband Bob who had a somewhat weary smile on his face making Charles Henry ask "What ya got there girls...a secret?" He assumed (and most probably rightly) *looks like those girls have been pulling that boy every which way but loose!*

"Ya'll look like the cat that ate the canary there, did ye find treasures?" he snickers.

His grown daughters had just returned from cleaning out the contents of his mother-in-law's home of over five decades. Upon their arrival home he could almost <u>feel</u> their anticipation! He knew they were highly excited about <u>something</u>! The girls noticed Pa's iced-tea glass looking pretty low there and waited for 'the sign.'

With a grin and a wink he held up his glass and shook the ice cubes within.

This particular movement on his part usually brought five women to their feet to refill their Daddy's glass over the years. This time would be no exception and Nola Jane went about refilling his beverage.

His favored spot on the old porch swing found him enjoying the bounties of his lovely home, the warm North Florida weather and the opportunity to just sit a spell. He was found most times in this spot if there were no errands to run or chores to complete.

His retirement had been very good to him and his love, Lois Marion.

Charles Henry was head of a household which contained a beautiful wife, one year and two months older than he but certainly no wiser in his mind. Even though his personality was one of much joviality and mirth and hers was quiet and ladylike, they were a totally matched pair. They could recount their histories together of many years of devotion one to the other.

Together they had raised four daughters and now in the twilight of their years enjoyed the husbands, children, and grandchildren visiting their lovely home on the lake. Life was very good for them now; the hardships of their former lives well behind them and they were finally able to slow down and watch the world go by...together.

They had lived, loved, worked hard, suffered injury and loss but also had been fortunate to enjoy their twilight years together. Their later years had brought many occasions of travel, cruises and visits to their daughters' homes in different locations over the years.

Calling to her Mama, Lois Marion, the oldest daughter, Dell Anne hollers "Mama, come look what we found in Grandmother's attic!" The girls had been busily checking and re-checking the home of the long widowed matriarch of the family, Lois Annie for items possibly left behind when she was forced to leave her home. Her advanced years and increasing ill health had forced a move to her daughter and beloved son-in-law's home this year of 1991.

She would no longer be able to live alone.

All the furniture had been removed and all corners, closets, cabinets, garages and any portion of the house that might contain a 'treasure' were thoroughly checked.

Dell Anne, eldest of the four 'cubs', first grandchild of Lois Annie and ten years older than Nola Jane, had spent much time with her beloved Grandmother over the years. As the first grandchild and much doted upon, every corner of this treasured little home had a memory contained therein.

Standing in the doorway reminiscing times gone by, Dell Anne relished the memories of favored pets and instances shared with her beloved Grandmother. She was saddened to think all those years of living alone in this beloved little abode were now gone and Lois Annie would have to rely on others for her care. Her grandmother had been fiercely independent her entire life but was also very relieved her beloved home would now be a new residence for her younger sister, Edna.

Lois Annie had suffered through the loss of two husbands; her first, Daniel Noonan passed this life three weeks after the birth of their daughter, Lois Marion. He had been all of twenty three years of age and she was a mere child of twenty. Their daughter was born the day before the Great Stock Market crash of 1929 which triggered the Great Depression and the hardships of the entire Nation were many during those years.

She had then married her second husband, had a second child, Clarence, Jr. then unfortunately lost Clarence, Sr. to World War II in 1945.

Many heart aches were suffered within this home, humble as it was but the love of those occupants from so long ago remained within as well.

Dell Anne was frightened for the health of her Grandmother but knew it was the best for all involved if Lois Annie moved into 'the house that love built', Charles Henry and Lois Marion's lakeside home.

Charles Henry had lost his own mother very early and treasured his Mother-in-law his entire life. He cared for her just as deeply as if she were his own.

His wife, Lois Marion, had always loved that particular trait in her husband; he was so giving and caring for her mother. Together the couple vowed to keep her mother safe and protected as long as they could.

This would be one thing they could do for her Mother and matriarch of the family in her twilight years. She would not be placed in a nursing home if they could help it. If the time came they needed live-in caretaking help, then so be it. They had plenty of room in that huge home and would assure Lois Annie's comfort as long as they could.

Lois Marion was standing at the kitchen sink when her daughters arrived and could tell her daughter was highly agitated.

With apprehension she asked her eldest "What's the matter; is there a problem?"

Short of breath in her enthusiasm, Dell Anne began "Well, Mama we found some 'treasures' in the attic at Grandmother's and we think it's something you thought was lost forever!"

Her curiosity piqued, Mama asks "Oh, what would that be?"

Her daughter replied "Well we found this really nice piece of an unfinished quilt up there hidden in the attic. We almost missed it but I persuaded Bob to get up there and look under the insulation. He found it right at the opening to the attic."

As they unfolded the beautiful pristine piece of hand-made quilting she said "Look, it's the quilt we worked on while Daddy was fighting in the War! I haven't seen that thing for years, have you Mother?"

Grandmother replied "Well, no, I had completely forgotten about that thing. Bring it over here honey, and let me look it over."

Dell Anne obediently took the thin package within which the treasure had been wrapped those oh so many years ago and gently unfolded the quilt.

Lois Marion cried out "Oh look Mother, there's the material from my favorite little dress you made all those years ago! And there's another one... and another one! I remember so many of those pieces of material you made our clothes with!"

Lois Annie replied "Well, yes, if you remember, those days were very hard and we had to use any and all material to make clothes, drying cloths and bedding. Nothing was wasted."

She continued sadly "This was the memory quilt we were making when Clarence, Sr. was sent to the war front and before we learned he had been killed."

She could no longer shed tears since her illness had left her without the ability to cry. If she could have she would have loved to shed just one for both of her lost husbands.

Dell Anne asked her Grandmother, "You know, this looks like it's ready to be completed. It looks like you completed the entire top; each little square looks to be completely sewn. Would you like for me to have it finished for you?"

With resignation the Matriarch of this family replied "I don't really have a use for it now and even though it's a treasure and shows all the hard work we put into it, I just don't think I could bear to have it around. It brings back way too many sad memories."

Dell Anne began refolding the quilt to place it back into its brown paper packing in which it had rested since 1945…a whole lifetime ago.

Turning to her Granddaughter she asks Dell Anne, "Would you like to have it honey? You're welcome to keep it if you like."

Totally overcome with the emotions garnered within the room Dell Anne replied "Oh yes, Grandmother, I would LOVE to have it. Thank you so much! My sister-in-law, Barbara is a talented quilter and I'll have it completed. It will have a forever home with me!"

With much interest, Lois Marion eyed a packet of letters tied with a little bow which appeared to have been with the forgotten quilt and asks "Is that what I THINK it is?"

Dell Anne and Nola Jane shared a glance and grinned "Yep…this looks like Daddy's letters you always told us about!"

With a shout Mama moved like 'greased lightning' (for which she was NOT known) and fingered the little package in her daughter's hand. She exclaimed "My heavens, over the years I've wondered where they were. With all the moves we've had over the years we just assumed they got lost. Aunt Doris kept them in an old coffee can for the longest time but I didn't remember where they went after a while. It was a horrible loss for me but I just figured there was no use crying over spilled milk!"

The daughters had initially thought the letters had belonged to their grandmother since there was previously another such package of letters retrieved. Those letters were the letters written by Lois Annie to her husband Clarence, Sr. but were never opened.

The sad fact was during the period of the hateful War, the notification of her husband's death was months in coming and the package returned to her contained the letters she had written to him, each stamped RETURN TO SENDER: DECEASED.

The initial assumption was these must have been more letters between their Grandparents. To their great excitement however they realized these in fact were the love letters written by their father, Charles Henry to their mother, Lois Marion all those long years ago and had not been lost at all!

The girls had been hesitant to open any of those letters; it was evident each had been unsealed, read then lovingly returned to their original envelopes many times over. They had decided they just didn't feel right intruding into their parents' love lives.

They would turn them over to their Mama and allow her the joy of re-reading her husband's love from all those many years before. (Both, however, would have loved to be a fly on the wall when their Daddy heard his own words read back to him!)

The couple had been married almost fifty years, celebrated many anniversaries together through good times and bad but had remained devoted one to the other.

Charles Henry had been watching this little scene and turned to his one and only love over all these years and said with a twinkle in his green eyes and a sweet smile on his lips, "I'm so sorry Baby Doll, I am sorry to tell you but over all these years I just didn't keep any of <u>YOUR</u> proof! I kept them for a time but I guess over the years, they just got misplaced...I have no idea where they are."

Lois Marion, excitedly fingered the little package and replied "That's okay Daddy, I remember each and every word I wrote to you in those letters; they have always lived in my heart. You have given me so much more than words in our lives together, I thank you. I'm just grateful I can re-read all of your sweetness and remember always!"

She also vowed *once these young'uns go home I'm going to read every one of these again!*

The afternoon was yet again a lovely sharing of family; Dell Anne, husband Naser, children, Bobby and Shaida and sister, Nola Jane and husband, Bob sharing yet again a family meal with their parents.

Those days were always treasured by all and Charles Henry was proud to have his 'cubs' return home at any time.

"Ya'll come on back and visit with us any time you want, girls!" he said, and meant every word of it.

The treasures found this day began a whirlwind of memories within the mind of this author, allowing the great privilege to read the words our Father had so long ago penned to his young love.

Once these words were witnessed, the wonder of just how sentimental and devoted he was to our Mother became crystal clear as never before. We always knew he was strong and generous, but never dreamed he possessed such writing skills, especially in something so private as love letters.

The general thought of his daughters on the subject of their Father's written words was that they might be on the order of "Hi, how are you...? Gotta go now!"

I am Dell Anne Hines Afzal, author of this tribute of love to my family and I offer a glimpse of a lifetime of memories and devotion from two very treasured members of my family: my Mama, Lois Marion and my Daddy, Charles Henry Hines.

My hope is that you take a little trip back in time to the beginning of our family story and enjoy this tribute of love and devotion.

The Wood Sawin',
North Central Florida, 1944

The sideboards were laden with steaming dishes of freshly prepared food. Neighbor families gathered at Grandma and Grandpa's farm to help the family chop wood for the winter. The fall days were growing increasingly shorter each day and World War II is in full swing in Europe.

The small north-central Florida rural community was busy at the wood sawin' at the old homestead.

It was customary for community members to gather together to share the burdens of farm work in preparation for the winter months. This occasion would bring the wood necessary to sustain the needs of the family for heating and cooking.

The area supported a veritable cornucopia of native trees for the various needs of the families. The community of farmers had no easily accessible metropolis in which to do their shopping. They had to travel ten miles north for staples but grew most of their own food.

These were farmers of tobacco, corn, watermelons, and peas and they raised their own hay to feed their livestock. This work required long daily hours spent feeding livestock, mending fences, and tilling the soil. Times were hard and lean and everyone did their fair share of work. They shared what they had in order to help their communities survive during those horrible war years.

Families came together to complete the manual labor necessary to keep farms running successfully. Males too young to be drafted for service into the war were especially proud to give of their strength and hard work to these families. Each family would reciprocate to the other thus ensuring the hard work could be accomplished for all. If someone needed help, there were always others ready to assist.

Our nation was a nation of patriotism, rationing, contributing what they could to fight an unseen, yet acknowledged enemy to keep our own shores safe from harm.

"Buy War Bonds" was the subject of many radio programs and enticements between the movie credits at the local picture show. Producers of metal goods such as cooking pots were asked to change their product lids from metal to glass. The precious metals were needed to make arms and other military equipment.

Young girls and women were challenged to work in factories, often taking the place of a man who had gone to war. The women took whatever job they could to help the war efforts.

Everyone saved what they could and prayed for the safety of their families and the nation. Each person knew to "count their blessings where they find em" and tried to live their lives in that manner.

Their beloved young military men and women would send letters back home to their families telling them of their travels-- if they could. Many times the Military would not allow them to inform their families of their exact locations. The soldiers and sailors attempted to show their loved ones at home they longed for home and their families. The separation was difficult for those left at home and those fighting the war.

Letters from home to the front were sometimes few and far between but they were the best mode of communication at that time in our history. Each family member looked forward to mail call whether at home or in service. The recipient read the words with much love and appreciation that the writer took the time out of his or her busy life to send a love note.

Most of these families depended on the income from the crops to survive. Many did not have day jobs to offer monthly or even yearly salaries. Everything grown on the farm provided the family's yearly income and food.

On this day in 1944, the sound of saws echoed through the woods as the young men chopped those large, old oak, sweet gum and any other trees that produced suitable wood for burning. Every home boasted a fireplace, and wood was treasured not only for the heat and warmth it gave to the home but was also the cooking fuel of choice. Each felled tree brought warmth and sustenance to the families.

In the distance, echoes of men warning that another tree was coming down were prevalent. Joyful sounds of children running wild and free were welcoming. Their sounds of laughter intermingled with the sounds of work going on around them.

Households often consisted of grandparents and their children, who in turn, had their own children. So the farm might support three or four family generations living on the same homestead.

Community members all greatly anticipated the wood sawin' since it would bring others together as a unit and offer a great source of comfort to everyone.

While the men felled trees and children played, women and young girls busily prepared a meal for the hungry workers. Besides the family of the farmer on whose land the sawin' was taking place, those who brought workers also prepared home- cooked dishes to share after the work had been completed.

The men constructed saw horses upon which to lay down simple wooden boards the width of those saw horses, effectively constructing huge tables. The tables were covered with all manner of colorful tablecloths, many hand-embroidered by the young women and grandmas. They were a great source of family pride.

Finally everyone partook of the simple country food after someone offered blessing to the heavens. "Lord, bless this food to the nourishment of our bodies and us to thy service," he would fervently intone. "Guide us and direct us through each day and Lord, please bless our loved ones fighting overseas. Bring them all safely back home to each and every one of us."

Everyone with heads bowed would whisper "Amen." The farmers and their families were proud God-fearing and loving individuals. They all knew how blessed they were to live in that day and time, albeit a time of great suffering to others in many parts of the world.

On the day of the wood sawin' the meal would consist of all manner of fresh canned food, since each family grew their own corn, peas, butterbeans, new potatoes, snap beans, tomatoes, cucumbers, okra, and squash. The bounty was proudly prepared, usually by the female members and children old enough to help. They spent long, hot hours gathering and preparing the vegetables for canning to support the family food requirements for the year.

Many front porches were graced with sweet potato vines and pole beans serving both as a vegetable field around the front of the house and to shelter the porch from the hot Florida sun. Residents of the homestead were sent to the front porch to pick the pole beans without ever having to leave the house.

These vines were highly prized as the landscaping greenery around the home since many residents did not allow their yards to grow grass. Many of the 'old-timers' still swept the dirt yards clean, removing all traces of grass and weeds, keeping the exterior of the home neat and tidy.

Watermelon rind pickles were canned from the sweet and plentiful watermelons grown each year. After the sweet fruit had been enjoyed and the rind scraped sufficiently, the leftover rind was mixed with sweeteners and spices to enjoy the rest of the year. During tobacco harvest, sticky nicotine tar would stain the hands of the workers and a watermelon might be sacrificed in which to wash. Watermelon juice is a wonderful natural cleansing product of nicotine tar and nothing would go to waste.

Tomatoes were mixed with okra and corn and canned as a special treat served over white rice. Silver Queen corn was creamed and canned. Cucumbers were cut and brined for salty pickles. They also prepared 'bread and butter' pickles which are so sweet and tasty.

Butter beans, white acre peas, purple hull peas, Crowder peas, and Texas Cream peas caused the families to gather together in the summer afternoons. Everyone shelled those pods to retrieve their luscious treats.

Families sat under old shade trees shelling peas and socializing with each other. There was no television, radio, or computer in sight.

Many of these farmers had saved pea or bean pods for subsequent crops thus continuing the treasured art of keeping "seed stock" from generation after generation.

They lovingly dried the seeds and imagined their great granddaddies beginning the stock. They were proud to continue the honored tradition.

A treasured seed stock could be the subject of many conversations bringing treasured memories of the homestead and former residents.

These treasures were revered as highly as any gold or silver.

"You know, those white acre peas over there have been grown from seed stock started by my Great Grandpa during the Civil War," someone might say. "He was so afraid somebody might take 'em, he buried 'em in a glass jar in the chicken yard." he might add.

Another member might agree and bring up his own family history of saved stock to create wonderful stories and memories for all to enjoy.

Meats served at these get-togethers were usually simple fare: ham, sausage, pork chops, fried chicken, rabbit, squirrel, deer, fried catfish and fresh water fish from the nearby Santa Fe River. There were also some of what today's society might consider more unusual meats, including beef tripe, liver, hog's-head cheese, and even possum if needed.

Nothing was discarded when it came to the family food requirements. There were no medical professionals warning them of health hazards during those times.

During the winter months, if the family had run out of their summer canned goods, they depended on winter vegetables, such as mustard, collard, and turnip greens. They were served with a skillet of cornbread for a simple but delicious meal.

The wood sawin' was a festive occasion of working, eating, and socializing. They all knew if they could help others, everyone would share the work again to help the next family as well—perhaps even their own.

It was at such a sawin' on a beautiful fall day in 1944 that a relationship began between two teenagers.

It was on this day that Lois Marion, age fourteen, and Charles Henry, age thirteen met.

This meeting began a lifetime of devotion and love.

The Young Man with Green Eyes

Charles Henry was a local lad whose father became a widower when the young son was only six years old. William Henry, Charles Henry's father, lost his young wife Ola Dell to a stroke following the birth of their youngest child, Juanita in 1936. This left William Henry with a twelve year old daughter, Maude, a six year old son, Charles Henry and a newborn infant, Juanita, and a strong determination to make a living as a share-cropper in their very humble home.

He was determined to assure his little family survived together.

The home in which they survived during difficult times was owned by a wealthy land owner and was offered in partial payment for William Henry's labors in the field. It was a hard life for the little family and all had to do their share of the work to survive.

William Henry put many long hard daylight hours into tilling the soil, always with a mule and plow, which was a back-breaking task to say the least. He suffered greatly with painful varicose veins although he could not allow this fact to affect his need to work long hard hours on his feet in the heat of the Florida sun.

The oldest daughter, Maude, shortly after her mother's death married an older neighbor man and together they started a new life in another town farther south, their chance for a new start.

At the tender age of six years old Charles Henry became the chief caretaker of his infant sister, Juanita and together they forged a lifetime bond. That bond was at times very tender and carefree as siblings but at others also tumultuous as they grew to maturity.

Much of the raising and caretaking duties had to be left to the young son since the father couldn't be in two places at once; both in the field and also in the home caretaking an infant.

Many times father and son would place Juanita in a vegetable crate at the end of the rows where she could hopefully sleep under the shade of the big oaks. Father and son plowed, hoed the young plants or harvested their bounty. As she became a toddler she sometimes was left alone under those shaded trees to play in the dirt.

Father would be nearby keeping watch as he toiled in the hot sun.

Charles Henry thoroughly enjoyed going to school and felt very fortunate his father allowed him to walk to the country school. However, even in his elementary years, the drudgery of the farm took all their waking hours. As soon as his little feet could walk the distance back home from school, he was expected to be in the field helping his father and looking after Juanita for whatever needs she might have.

Thus, the young man entered into the teenaged years but learned all those lessons of hard work and determination at a very high cost to his own childhood.

The neighbors would commend William Henry on how hard his young son worked and what a precise and thorough job he did with anything he attempted. His recommendations were very high with the older farmers in the area and his opinions were well respected by his elders. He made it his business to learn all he could about his chosen field, that of farming the soil. He studied hard in school excelling in his studies, especially mathematics and agriculture.

He was also known as the class joker with a very clever, quick and dry wit and loved to laugh. He especially loved to tease; his sparkling green eyes considered very charming to many. He made friends easily and forged lifetime friendships with many.

During his high school years, he was a much respected class member and even though the class was very small and team players were few, he played basketball with his buddies whenever the chance might present itself. His good friends, G.W., Ralph G, Frank, Leon and Ralph F were close and all loved those chances to socialize, even if it meant they would have to work hard before they could do so.

It was on this day in 1944 the wood sawin' would offer an opportunity for a very witty young man with twinkling green eyes to meet a black haired, shy young lady and a future together would be forged.

Charles Henry, the young man with the green eyes was the ripe old age of thirteen years.

That Pretty little 'City Girl'

Lois Marion was a pretty little black eyed, black haired beauty who even at the age of fourteen was beginning to show signs of becoming a beautiful woman. Her confidence suffered greatly at this age however keeping her quiet, shy and retiring. Her mother, Lois Annie taught her the manners of a lady from the very start of her life.

Lois Marion was very kind and gentle and not prone to raising her voice, especially in anger; that just was NOT done in her world. She was well liked by her friends and classmates.

She began life under tragic circumstances, losing her twenty three year old father, Daniel Noonan to a rare disease when she was only three weeks old. She was born on the day after the Stock Market fell in 1929 and that time in our world was a dark time indeed.

Her twenty year old mother, Lois Annie was forced to return to her childhood home with her mother, Eva Marion and father Sidney, Sr., and a 'host' of siblings. The family held an extremely large and boisterous group of boys and girls and many of the fourteen were quite rambunctious to say the least.

Eva Marion and Sid., Sr. would welcome their fifteenth and last child, Harold into the family after the birth of his oldest sister's child, Lois Marion. This fact made him an Uncle to Lois Marion even before he was born.

Twelve of the fifteen children would maintain long and fruitful lives; however three would not survive their infancies.

Lois Marion grew to love her mother's siblings and lived with that family until around the age of three. Even though shy and quiet, in order to survive in that rowdy household she was forced to become a little more outgoing during that time.

Around the age of three her mother, Lois Annie, widowed at the tender age of twenty, met and married a young man, Clarence, Sr., and Lois Marion gained a step-father. He moved his new little family to the northernmost side of the county away from her beloved Aunts and Uncles whom she considered more like brothers and sisters.

They moved into a home owned by a local attorney and Clarence, Sr. became a share cropper for the attorney on the large tract of land far removed from neighbors.

During this time Lois Marion had terrible fears of the old dark house in which they lived and began tailing her mother at every turn, so afraid was she in that dark place. For the first year of their time in this home, she would not leave her mother's skirt-tails.

Visitors coming to call would most times see a tiny little raven-haired girl with tiny little coal black eyes staring around her mother's skirt-tails. Most times, any greeting or cajoling of those visitors to speak with her would be frightfully ignored by the little girl.

Eventually Lois Annie and Clarence Sr. presented Lois Marion with a new little brother, Clarence, Jr., and she began to realize she could be open and playful with another child again, even if he was younger and smaller than she. After all, she was now a big sister. Her years in school brought her confidence a little higher but her shyness remained somewhat of a problem for some time.

On this glorious fall day in 1944 at the home of her Step-Grandparents, the young ladies busily placed the colorful tablecloths over the primitive wooden side boards and excitedly exchanged glances with one another. Most certainly while conducting their chores, many were checking out the available young men working that day as well.

Her young cousins were checking out the platters of food and arranging the respective dishes at the proper locations. The meats were together in one place, all the vegetables in another and most especially the dessert dishes in a favorite location.

They were hostesses of the social and would be required to assure the success of the meal as much as the mother and grandmother of the homestead.

Lula Mae, Regina and Jackie were the three daughters of her stepfather's twin, Clara and were very close with Lois Marion all during her young life. The reunions of the families would bring great times of friendship and were longingly anticipated by all. The girls, even though not in the same classes or even the same school all treasured each other.

Lois Marion attended school in town and was considered that 'city girl' while the sisters all attended the country school where Charles Henry and his buddy, Ralph G also attended. Jackie and Charles Henry's youngest sister, Juanita were great friends all during their youth as well.

Lula Mae and Lois Marion were more of an age than Regina and Jackie but all were close. The three sisters were much more outgoing and open to strangers than shy and retiring Lois Marion. However, the sisters didn't allow her shyness to impact their fun in any way.

All the girls were busily working but each in their own right was aware of the young men who would presently be served the wonderful meal after a hard day's work.

The sounds of the trees being felled and the sawing and chopping of the wood resounded throughout the countryside. The fruits of the labors of a hard day of work would soon be rewarded with sustenance, friendship and fun.

On this day in 1944, Lois Marion, the young black haired shy young lady was about to become fifteen years old and was ready and anxious to learn her future, whatever may come.

The Beginning

Charles Henry was busy sawing and chopping the wood with all of his young friends. Even though he had not grown to his fully mature adult body, he was strong as an ox and not afraid of hard work. Thus, he dug his heels in and cut all the wood he could before time to go the house and partake of the wonderful covered dish dinner awaiting them.

When he began cleaning up a little in preparation for those great dishes he noticed out of the corner of his eye a very tiny black haired girl with tiny coal black eyes and thought he recognized her from another time and place.

He wasn't sure if it was the same girl he remembered from another time; *if so, she sure has grown up nicely* he thought.

Lois Marion was preparing the tables for lunch and noticed his striking green eyes as well.

They had noticed each other in former times but it appears the occasion just never arrived for them to actually speak to each other before. However, now they were thirteen and fourteen and we all know at that age interest in the opposite gender begins to spark. This certainly was the case on this day in 1944.

He was still young enough to be playful, slapping at his friends and running barefoot down the dirt road, tossing the balls at the other boys and playing whatever games they could play while awaiting their meal.

All the while he was playing, surreptitiously his gaze would move to her quiet form and if she caught his eyes on her he would quickly jump back into play with his buddies.

During the meal, this little cat and mouse game would be played and she would wonder in her own mind… *He is sooooo handsome, why haven't I noticed him before?* She was quite taken with his prowess both in play and strength.

One trait she did not cherish, however, was his penchant for tobacco. He was no different from many of the young men in those days who worked in the tobacco field. He partook of the bounty of the fields and rolled his own cigarettes. The time in our history proves movie stars were more often than not sporting the cigarette as a symbol of strength, beauty and wealth. It was no wonder the masses idolized the habit. We now know much more about the hazards of smoking that plant.

Lois Marion however, did not like the habit because of the smell it left upon the person of a smoker.

Lula Mae and Regina noticed the quick and furtive glances at the young man with the green eyes. Lula Mae whispered "look, she's looking at him again."

"Yes", Regina would comment, "he's checking her out too. Wouldn't it be something if they liked each other? Maybe we can try to get them together after the meal when we start playing games" they schemed. "Let's see, we can play spin the bottle; maybe that will put them together. Who knows, it's certainly a chance and if that bottle stops on one of them they HAVE to do what the game demands" they whispered secretly.

The afternoon wore on and soon became time for the men to clean up for the much anticipated vittles which were sure to be covering those groaning side-boards set up as dining tables.

Whoops of joy and excitement filled the air when the community came to the tables and all prepared for the offering of Prayer. All heads bowed and the prayer was sent up with all present feeling the pleasure of the moment. Many silently hoped the prayer-giver would not be too long this time since the hunger pangs would be silently but surely roiling throughout the crowd.

With the blessing complete and all "Amens" sent heavenward, the attendees began lining up to partake of the simple but luscious bounty set before them.

The workers usually ate first as the manual labor left them many times in a weakened state. The mothers would help the little ones with their plates in hopes they settled quietly soon. Some might move the elders forward to the front of the line in respect for advanced years. No one was in fear there would be no food left for them once they got to their places in line; there was plenty for all.

It was at this time Lula Mae and Regina began their efforts at moving Lois Marion closer to Charles Henry in hopes of striking up a new acquaintance.

Who knows what else might happen from this meeting?

"Hey, Ralph, why don't we get our plates and sit over there near those girls?" Charles Henry whispered. "I'd like to meet that girl with the black hair. I really like the way she looks" he said with a grin. *Her hair is really pretty with all those bouncy, black curls. I wonder if she notices me...* he thought to himself.

From his friend, Ralph G. "That younger sister, Regina looks great to me! I've been seeing her at school and this just might be the time to talk to her." Ralph commented with mischief in his eyes. "I'm checking out that one for myself!"

Charles Henry finds his way over to Lois Marion and introduces himself "Hi, I'm Charles, what's your name?" he asks.

She blushes prettily and quietly answers "I'm Marion, pleased to meet ya."

With more courage now, the young man asks "Where do you go to school? How old are you?"

"Well, I'll be fifteen at the end of this month and I go to school in town. Do you go to school out here in Mason with my cousins?" she asked.

Quickly he answers "Yep, I turned fifteen in June of this year and yeah, I go to Mason. I guess we have something in common, don't we?"

The conversation stalls as they shyly wonder who would be the next to communicate.

"Well, I guess I'd better get back to Ralph and see what he's up to. See ya later maybe?"

She only smiled prettily at him and watched him leave her side knowing she must get busy with serving and making sure the hostess duties were accomplished. Yet she remained rooted to her spot not wanting to miss one glance of him...

Charles Henry located his friend Ralph who had expressed an interest in Regina previously and together they get in line to be served their lunch. He noticed that Ralph was mightily interested in watching that pretty little Regina...

Regina was three years younger than Lula Mae and Lois Marion and would tire soon of the game of match making since there might be other more interesting games to play later.

Of course, it might be at this time that Regina herself might have slanted her eyes at a certain member of the young male duo herself...

The Games Children Play

All during the meal, Charles Henry is glancing over at Lois Marion and wondering just how to approach the young girl. Does he get close to her and trip her up like some young men seem to think is the way to a girl's heart?

No, he thinks to himself, *I don't think she would appreciate that. That doesn't seem to be the way. How about this,* he thinks. *Do I just walk straight up and ask her to sit with me?* As he continues enjoying his food, he notices every once in a while she lifts her head ever so slightly and surreptitiously glances his way.

He wonders to himself *Wow…is she interested in me too or do I have food on my face?*

In her own mind she is wondering if she just might have a chance with this handsome young man with the striking green eyes. *Oh dear,* she thinks, *is he interested in me? I know Mother would be very upset if I just go over and talk to him. She always told me not to be forward; a girl has to wait for the boy to make the first move!*

She worries and frets slowly chewing her meal but winds up merely playing with it.

The meal progressed and when all had been satiated, the time came to put away the leftover food, tables and benches. Chores completed, the time arrives for games and conversation. Now everyone can just enjoy the time together.

The women and girls completed their respective tasks and the children began to choose up sides for games and merriment. Dusk is falling and the fires are lit. Night is coming and everyone is tired but unwilling to give up the frivolities just yet.

This night is a celebration of life and friends!

A game once called 'Spin the Bottle' seems to be a very important rite of passage in the small communities and generations have played it for years.

The young boys and girls would stand in a large circle and first up would be chosen to spin a bottle in the sand. When the bottle stopped spinning, it would point to another of the group, preferably of the opposite gender. The point of the game would be an introduction of sorts and would require the couple to walk together down a specific path then return.

These walks would be monitored by the older of the Mamas and Grandmas and would require the youngsters to take minimum time in their 'return to the fold' so to speak. Everyone must be on their best behavior; however, many lifetime commitments were forged in these young and seemingly innocent games.

On this evening, Lois Marion was the one player 'up' to spin the bottle. In her young and innocent mind, hopes of the chance of the bottle's pointed end aligning with Charles Henry surely crossed her mind. Quietly and hopefully she spins the bottle and stands back...

In her soul she prays *Oh spinning bottle, please give me a chance to talk with that boy!*

She takes a deep breath, closes her eyes and spins the bottle.

While watching that spinning bottle, Charles Henry in his own right is wishing it would land on his person as well. He thought *this would be the perfect way to talk with this beautiful girl!* With absolute amazement he realized the bottle HAS stopped at him. *Wow...can you believe it? IT'S POINTING TO ME!*

Lois Marion is almost sick with anticipation and fear as well as she realizes her dream has come true! The bottle actually landed at her intended's feet!

Now she must follow through and go for that walk with him!

She worried *how in the world will my trembling legs support me and how can I possibly carry on a real conversation with him? I am just plain SCARED!*

If the firelight and lack of sunshine could have revealed the coloring in both their cheeks that night, one realizes they most certainly would have been blushing bright red at their respective changes of luck!

As the lively and boisterous group screams with delight at the young couple, they push Lois Marion and Charles Henry together with demands to get on the way for that walk!

The young couple was only too glad to comply!

(One would have loved to be a fly on the wall at the conversation or lack thereof which might have transpired during that walk.) She would have been concerned they might be taking too long and didn't want her Mother to worry about her, yet she wanted to spend as much time as possible with him. Besides, she was embarrassed to tears she was alone with a young man and had no idea how to handle the next few minutes.

He, on the other hand, would have been dreaming of getting to know her better as well; *just how?* He also didn't want to ruin his chances since he already had designs on this little 'City Girl.'

The conversation was small, embarrassed and lacking but at their return to the group, it was just enough to allow Charles Henry's continued presence at Lois Marion's side the rest of the evening.

Both youngsters relished the moments with joy and happiness!

Neither would remember much of the games that night, only of the respective nuances of the other and desires to see one another again. Both left the evening's festivities with much reluctance but also with much anticipation of the next meeting. (One imagines both probably dreamed of their futures whether only for a few days, months or possibly for a lifetime, if youngsters their ages COULD dream of lifetime futures. After all, this WAS wartime...)

The Kerosene Stove

In the following weeks, Charles Henry was disgusted he had not had the nerve to actually ask Lois Marion out on a date the night of the wood sawin'. He wasn't really of an age to do so and neither was she. However he felt the need to seek her out once again.

He devised a plan to find out where she lived, see her in her own family surroundings and hopefully bring favor with her family.

During the time of the community festivities he had a mutual friend who knew Lois Marion and also where the family lived. Charles Henry learned of this after querying his friend and came up with a plan to have his friend show him exactly where she lived. He was in hopes of devising a plan to ask her out if her family would allow it.

Neither family had a telephone in those days to alert the other to a prospective meeting. Saturday morning came and he and his friend hitch-hiked their way into town early in the morning to witness the location of his new love's home.

His friend who had done his duty to point out the location of her home disappeared leaving Charles Henry to gather all his courage to knock on Lois Marion's front door alone.

(In later years, Charles Henry would admit to his family, "I have no idea where he went…he just disappeared! I didn't even care where he went; I just knew I had found her!")

Charles Henry marched with determined steps to her front door and soundly rapped on the door.

Lois Marion, who in the early Saturday morning hours had her entire head sunk into the old kerosene oven cleaning out the filth wonders, *who in the world would be knocking on our door at this hour?*

Forgetting she has her hair tied up in a bandana, with certain soot smudges all over her face and arms realizes she is alone in the house and as such must be the one to open the door in greeting. She has no time to check her appearance in the mirror but could only remove the gloves used to protect her hands from cleaning the sooty aftermath of cooking in a kerosene oven. She forgot to untie her filthy apron from around her waist and ran to the door.

In her horror she realized there stood her love from afar, that boy with the green eyes she had so long dreamed of since their last meeting at the wood sawin'.

With much pleasure but also much alarm at her present appearance, she wonders how he had he found her house. Her next thought is *Oh my Lord, I have my hair all tied up and I'm stinky and filthy from the stove, how can he possibly want to see me this way? I'll just die right here and right now!*

Charles Henry however, so relieved to know he had found her home and was here speaking with her in person, didn't even care she was covered head to toe in soot. He just was too pleased to see her!

He stammered out his first words "Hello...I was just wondering...would you want to go to the picture show with me this afternoon? I mean...if you don't want to, I'll understand. I just thought you might like to see a movie today..."

With a red face and his heart in his throat he awaits her answer, fearing the worst "NO" he has ever feared in his life!

She, with her likewise red and blushing cheeks replies "Well, YES, I'd love to go!"

"You do...I mean, you WILL?" he stammered. "Do you have to ask your Mother if you can go? I mean...is she here?"

Lois Marion normally would have absolutely asked her Mother's permission in an event of this magnitude but on this the most wonderful day of her life made an executive decision...she WOULD go with this green-eyed young man. She would NOT wait to ask for permission either; thank you very much!

Her heart soared he had found her and lost all embarrassment of her dirty appearance or even asking how he found her home.

It was of no consequence.

The only thing that mattered at that moment was he was here and he HAD asked her out! She was as high on adrenaline as any time she could remember in her life! She didn't even have time to worry if her Mother would approve or give permission at that moment, it didn't even matter. She would take care of that at a later time...right NOW she was going to say YES!

Charles Henry, now relieved he had gained the courage to ask the first question stood at her front door. He no longer knew what next to say and could only respond. "Well, I'll see you this afternoon...I'll be back."

She agreed and remained in the doorway watching her new love walk down the street, never asking him where he would go to wait for their approaching date nor what he would do. She only knew she HAD to finish cleaning the filthy oven and with haste set about accomplishing the task at hand.

She worried the approaching time would not allow her to wash her hair so prayed it looked presentable once she took it out of the bandana. She began to plan what 'frock' she would wear for the upcoming event.

Once apprised of this new development in her daughter's life, Lois Annie was quite impressed at the presence of mind and determination the young man had shown to seek out her daughter. She happily agreed Lois Marion would be allowed to go to the picture show with him. She set about helping her daughter prepare for the Saturday afternoon meeting. She already knew of his family and the hardships suffered in the loss of his mother. She also knew of father and son's reputations in the community as being hard-working, honest and good men. She was proud her daughter had seen something of interest in a young man of his caliber. She also remembered her own first love and how wonderful those new and exciting feelings were.

Lois Marion did not have the time to wash, roll and dry her hair since it normally took an entire afternoon or overnight for her long, very thick black hair to dry sufficiently. She could not go with wet hair; she'd look like a drowning cat!

She opted to hope for the best knowing she at least had possessed the presence of mind to cover her long hair with the bandana while cleaning the stove. She primped, assuring her dress was perfectly pressed and shoes were gleaming white.

All through her school years she had a penchant for making sure her saddle oxford shoes were perfectly polished white each evening and she was immaculately clean and neat at all times.

On one hand she was secretly pleased to wear the moniker "the girl with the white shoes" from her classmates however, on the other hand it embarrassed her that classmates would talk about her at all. In any event, she was perfectly groomed for her anxiously awaited young man's arrival.

Charles Henry arrived at the appointed time and was exceptionally pleased to recognize *Man…she cleans up real nice!* He was even more tickled to know she had accepted his invitation.

He was one proud young man that day!

He respectfully greeted Lois Annie and reintroduced himself to her younger brother, Clarence, Jr., who at the time thought it was wonderful his older sister might be gaining a boyfriend.

A very nervous young man agreed to protect Lois Annie's daughter, most especially the appointed curfew and they went on their merry way to the picture show.

The community theatre was not far from their residence and since the most favored mode of transportation in those days was foot traffic, they walked the distance. The local Court House, Post Office, City Park and a lovely lake were all adjacent to the theatre so there was activity most times of the day, weekdays and weekends as well.

(One might imagine yet another strained silence on this trip, each in his or her own imagination speaking what they knew they wanted to say to the other but neither having the courage to openly speak. It must have made for a very long but exciting walk together.)

Once they arrived at their destination, Charles Henry paid for entrance to the theatre and together they entered the building. Before entering the auditorium however, they needed to pass by the snack bar where he offered to buy her a treat before the movie started.

He asks "Would you like a *Coke* and popcorn before we go inside?"

In her mind, knowing of his supposed lack of funds and how hard for his family it had been responded "No thanks, I'm not really hungry." She knew in her heart her nerves would not allow her stomach to accept anything at the moment anyway!

He decides to go ahead and buy one drink and a bag of popcorn. He thinks *maybe she will get hungry and share with me later*. After making his purchase he ushers her into the darkened auditorium and with her acceptance finds an appropriate seat for them. They settled pleasantly together in preparation for the film to start.

The *Buy War Bonds* advertisements were shown, the Nation's admonishments to save aluminum and metal for the war mechanisms then the credits for the theatre rolled past. Clips of the USO shows being put on by celebrities overseas were shown to those back home as well to prove their soldiers were not ALWAYS fighting. Sometimes there were pleasures gained for our fighting soldiers in that hateful time of war.

During the showing of the films, Charles Henry was a gentleman even though he probably did not want to be. He also remembered the promise to Lois Annie of his protection for her daughter. After all, he was a man of his word.

Lois Marion could only enjoy his closeness in hopes he liked her as much as she liked him. They spoke in close whispers protecting the silence for the surrounding movie-goers. Most certainly they just enjoyed the other's close proximity. Young love is so very sweet.

During the progression of the afternoon, Lois Marion began to be aware of a pungent odor somewhere within their proximity. She couldn't exactly place the source but it seemed vaguely familiar. She would be too embarrassed to ask her young date if he could smell it as well so chose to remain quiet enjoying their closeness. She would gain small whiffs of the odor at times but just could not bring it to her mind.

All at once while he was closely whispering into her ear yet another tidbit, she experienced another slight whiff and realized with horror that the pungent odor she smelled was her own hair!

In her haste to prepare for their date she had made a conscious choice NOT to wash her hair because of the length of time necessary to roll, set and dry it. Now she was slowly but surely paying the price for her decision! Shewas mortified!

In horror she worried *what can I say…can HE smell that soot from the filthy oven on me … have I been stinking of that foul smell all afternoon?* How in the world could she admit she knew it was her own hair reeking there in the theatre and could anyone else around them smell it as well? She became totally and absolutely paralyzed with fear how he could possibly NOT know it was his own date smelling so badly!

She finally garnered enough courage to ask him "Charles…can you smell that soot on me still? I didn't have time enough to wash my hair for our date today and I didn't realize it smelled so bad until now. I feel terrible!"

With his head close to hers, he whispered into her ear "I thought you probably didn't have time to wash your hair and yes, I could smell it but I just don't care…It doesn't matter one bit. I'm just proud to be here with you!"

It might have been at this very moment she truly fell in love with this green eyed young man. In his kindness and gentleness he had completely ignored an obvious problem on her part; and surely he must be more interested in her than she could ever have dreamed or hoped for!

They enjoyed the movie that afternoon and as they strolled back to her home afterwards she vowed she would retain the joy in her heart of this closeness for years to come.

When arriving to her door, he asked her "Do you think you might want to go out with me again sometime?"

He held his breath in anticipation of a possible negative response.

"Of course, I would LOVE to, thank you very much!"

He bid farewell at her door and left his new love dreamily watching him leave her home.

Both youngsters would be in total dreamland, each marveling at the new and exciting emotions stirring within and anxiously hoping for a next meeting.

Her future was brighter and more promising than any time in her young life!

(One wonders if HIS feet ever touched the ground all the way home!)

Courting

The wood sawin' had been held at the homestead of Lois Marion's step-grandparents and during the next few months Lois Annie made sure her children knew and kept in contact with as many of the community families as possible over those war years.

This fact made Charles Henry only too sure his new love would be a part of the next community gathering. Lois Marion was keen to attend those gatherings as well!

Their afternoons of attending the picture show were sometimes few and far between but the community get-togethers afforded the opportunity for the youngsters to see each other as often as possible in those months of World War II.

The young man pretty well kept his mouth shut to his friends that he now had a 'City Girl' in his mind. Even his buddies would not hear much from him on his growing interest in the raven haired beauty from town.

What thoughts ran through his young mind while playing basketball, accomplishing his mind-numbing chores in the fields or sitting in the classroom during this time? Surely they must have been concentrated on his new love.

Lois Marion was a keen artist and loved to doodle in her notebook all manner of cartoons, swirls and words at any time. Most certainly her doodles must have included his name while she was in the classroom and when alone in her room as well.

As many young girls also may remember there were and still are certain word games played over generations of crossing off like-letters of a couple's names gradually telling the story of a possible match being made. Some of these silly childish games might produce a match; most of the time, not so much.

In this particular case, however, if Lois Marion HAD been playing any of those match-making games, history might prove a match after all!

World War II was in full swing and those left behind in the communities while the men of the families were off in the trenches, had their lives impacted in many ways back home as well. Many shortages of goods and services and a general unease over the world stage were experienced by all.

Every community in this great nation was impacted in one way or another by the ravages of war, either by shortages or by the dreaded telegrams from the State Department of War notifying families of loss or injury of their loved ones.

The communities were bombarded with signs of the need for saving goods, rationing of gas, sugar and many everyday items which we take for granted today. Housewives were instructed to search for recipes to make the normal day to day meals for their families minus those rationed goods.

They were encouraged to develop new ways to cook their regular recipes without the short-supplied sugar, eggs, butter, milk and flour. Those farm families did not usually have the same shortages of eggs, milk and butter as the townsfolk since the farm livestock many times supported those needs. However, they did suffer in the absence of the sugar everyone wanted to use in preparing the luscious desserts popular in those days. Of necessity, they had to be content to substitute sugar cane and honey popular in this area of North Central Florida.

Searches of the internet today prove the existence of these old fashioned recipes and are treasured by many. Those recipes were willingly shared among the housewives of the time and many have ultimately evolved into some of our low-sugar, low-whatever recipes of today.

Everyone had to do their fair share of rationing and saving all they could and all learned to pray for the end to the War as soon as possible. During those hard times, however life also had to continue for the youngsters of the day making them more eager to begin their lives in hopes of a brighter day and future.

At the same time the thoughts were prevalent of the approaching ages of the young men and the possibility of being drafted into military service. Some young men were anxious to arrive at the draft age in order to fight in the War while the young women worried if their boyfriends would return at all.

Mothers and fathers worried of the whole situation on a daily basis since war seemed to be everywhere. Life, however, must go on as normally as possible for everyone.

The community stores usually closed their doors at 12:00 noon on Wednesdays and Saturdays. All who could would travel to 'town' and do their Saturday morning shopping; many times remaining to attend the showing of the weekly movie shows so popular at the time.

Radios were the primary means of entertainment but if the residents of the community had the means, they would try to attend the picture shows as much as possible. The afternoon matinee would be attended by teenagers as much as they could afford or dared.

Many Saturday afternoons were also times of meeting friends in the City Park and just being together.

As Charles Henry grew into his teenaged years, his full attention began to be focused on getting his work done early. As his little sister Juanita grew, father William Henry realized his young son needed to get away from his chores, school and his caretaker duties to just be a young man.

It was with this knowledge of his son's need in his heart William Henry allowed Charles Henry to find his way to town periodically to 'court' his new young love, Lois Marion.

The community of Mason City was quite a distance from town and neither father nor son owned a car. Thus, it was necessary for the young man to either hitch-hike a ride from a resident passing down 441 toward town or to purchase a Greyhound bus ticket to town. In those days, it was relatively safe for individuals to hitch rides and many youngsters had no reservations in doing so.

His first choice was to attempt to hitch a ride, since he could save his hard-earned coinage for the picture show. He was a very thrifty spender and saved every penny he could get his hands on to treat his girl to a movie. He was certainly not above doing without something he needed or wanted in order to save his pennies.

The landowner knew this young man was always eager to do any and all work for a little spending money and the youngster never turned down the opportunity to make extra money. He also respected the young man's motto of "a good day's work for a good day's pay" as well.

If he felt he had enough money for his bus tickets and an afternoon at the movies, then he might splurge and buy tickets both into town and back home again as well. In some cases, however, he would be forced to hitch-hike and walk both ways.

The walk BACK home was not nearly as difficult as the walk TO town since he also didn't want to disappoint Lois Marion's afternoon or his own. The imperative was to get TO her as promptly as possible.

On those afternoons, she anxiously awaited her new boyfriend, (this time with no remaining odors of soot) poised to enjoy yet another Saturday with her young man.

The routine was that he would arrive at her door at the appointed hour; they walked to the theatre (now holding hands whenever possible) and enjoyed the afternoon show. Most of the time she still refused his offer of a *Coke* and popcorn; she didn't want to assume he had money. After all, he was a very proud young man.

She quietly declined and when he offered her a little of his own, she would often partake, but only a little.

She always worried how he was going to get home; *would he have the money to take the bus or would he yet again hitch-hike?*

They held hands in the movie seats and whispered closely but quietly enjoying each other's company. At the end of the movie, they began their trek back to her home by foot still holding hands. She was rewarded with a kiss at her front door when he left.

After his date he began his long trek back home, on foot hitch-hiking or by bus back to the rural community.

Sunday arrived and each attended church in the morning. Afternoons were spent by each writing letters to the other. This would happen each and every Sunday for the endurance of their courting days whether they had physically seen each other that week or not.

Monday found the Post Office courier retrieving their respective letters and Tuesday would find each receiving yet another treasured letter from the other.

Tuesdays were to be treasured and exciting days for years to come...

Charles and Marion's first picture taken together

School Days in Mason City

During his tenure in the rural community school of Mason City, all students attended the same school building in notably small class sizes.

Charles Henry and Juanita attended the school and both were successful students. He had made his place known both in basketball and softball even though the classes did not offer an overabundance of players for any given sport.

The teachers of the school, however, were able to afford more personal attention to each student and would sometimes be able to take one or two students under their wings to develop certain skills or attributes. All teachers were willing to help their youngsters.

The community was a very large farming community and everyone had an experienced hand in growing crops and caring for farm animals. However, Charles Henry excelled in his sharing of information and skills to others. One of his teachers determined this skill needed to be expounded upon.

G.W. was his close friend and both excelled in their skills and willingness to share, both having won Future Farmers of America awards for their work. Both young men were held to high standards by their teacher and began to develop skills towards careers in farming. G.W. planned to attend the University of Florida in a nearby community.

Charles Henry, however, had no plans to attend college since there would be absolutely no tuition funds to help while he studied. He knew his limitations at that time and knew William Henry could not take money from Juanita's needs or his own to help his son attend college.

He absolutely understood his lot in life but also knew in his heart whatever future was in store for him and his love of Lois Marion, he would have to do it with the sweat of his own brow and most certainly NOT from a college education.

He determined to excel wherever he could.

During his time in high school, he also had been fortunate enough to obtain work in the rural school where he attended classes. At the age of fifteen he served in a permanent position as school custodian but had to keep his classes up as well.

It was the first time the little family had garnered a steady pay check and he was proud of his ability to share it with his father and sister. His normal duties during the cold weather included chopping wood and preparing the wood stoves for the students' comfort during classes. His day would begin well before dawn and of course the winters were hardest.

Even though this little North Central Florida community was in the 'South', we also sometimes experience many harsh and cold winters as well. After classes he could be found sweeping out and cleaning up each and every room after everyone left for the day.

Spring and fall days were not nearly so difficult in the early morning hours but there would be many days of stifling heat in the drudgery of his cleaning duties. During the summers of course, there would be no school attendance and he would miss that steady pay check. He would actively seek work with other land owners in cropping, unloading tobacco barns and performing the back breaking jobs associated with tobacco farming.

During this time, he also found time to make sure his father's obligations in the field were seen to as well. William Henry was still a share cropper and his money would not come until the end of the growing season when his crop was sent to market and he and the landowner could settle up.

Times were hard indeed.

The young son also found time to help out at home and play sports when he could. He was a very busy young man.

During these years his joy in receiving the awards and acceptance of his teachers and peers in his farming abilities proved to be a much treasured asset for the young man. He was honored to be asked by his teacher to speak at a special State-wide event in another town to other Future Farmers of America students and school personnel.

His normal delivery of information was clever, witty with charming anecdotes and analogies and with seeming very little effort to others. (Secretly, one wonders how he was able to speak in front of others; he must have gained much courage in the years since first meeting his young love, Lois Marion.)

His friend, G.W. was also chosen to deliver a speech and together they would be privileged to attend the State-wide convention as a team. During the planning of the event, a problem occurred in that the two speakers would not be able to present; only one would be able to do so for this time. Charles Henry bowed out, accepted his award and G.W. took his place.

In later years, G.W. went on to excel in his studies at the University of Florida, beginning in the agricultural field but later in life turned to the Seminary of which he would later make his entire career as a Pastor of the Gospel.

Charles Henry counted G.W. as a best friend from the start of their first grade meeting and lasted until the end of his time on earth.

Lois Marion's life had been spent in a farming family and she had known the hard work necessary to survive, not to mention the hardships of waiting to gather then sell the yearly crop for their family finances.

She wanted no part of the farm life and hoped her love would not choose to continue farming as a career. They were still very young but both had been through hardships during their courting days and experienced heartaches which would change the course of their futures in many more ways than one.

The Boys Learn SEX Education

During the school years of the youngsters, both Charles Henry and Lois Marion continued their friendships with school pals and kept their friendships strong.

Charles Henry worked his job at the school house, kept his studies up and tried to focus on his relationship with his young girlfriend. However, he was still close with his pals at school and played as many sports with them as possible. His close buddy was G.W. who lived a few miles further from town than Charles Henry.

The war was in full swing but these youngsters were too young to enlist for duty.

They both had been raised on the farm and knew many of the 'facts of life' from witnessing nature with the farm animals. However, boys at this young age had a natural attraction to nature and the actual experience of procreation; in other words...S E X.

The local picture show was going to be showing all manner of information on the war front on what the citizens of our country could be doing to help the war effort. The boys learned there was to be a showing on what soldiers being sent to foreign countries might expect when they were off duty.

There were warnings of what might happen if the young soldiers met foreign 'working women' and how to protect themselves. The news of this showing spread like wild fire in the town and every young man wanted to go to that movie...their curiosity was highly piqued on just how much information might be shared.

Of course, this would NOT be the kind of movie he would take Lois Marion to so it would be up to G.W. and himself to find their way to town for this one. Charles Henry didn't really need to ask permission since he sometimes took his girl to the picture show and his father had no reason to ask what picture was showing.

On the day the movie was to be shown, G.W. started walking toward town and met up with Charles Henry. Together they walked and thumbed their way into town to discover life or at least what they HOPED they might discover.

It was exciting at any rate!

Once in the theatre they realized there were MANY young men there and got their popcorn and drinks early so they wouldn't miss anything. The 'Roll Film' signs started the moving pictures, the necessary war announcements were played and the songs and dancing began.

As they sat anxiously awaiting to find out just how far that movie would go and how MUCH information would be shared, their total focus was centered on that movie screen.

How in the world will they show this? Each young man pondered.

They had seen the mating rituals of the cattle, horses, goats and all manner of farm animals but just couldn't fathom what would be shown. They were relieved this showing had been presented somewhat as a 'men only' viewing. Of that they were much relieved; there would be way too much embarrassment if there were girls in attendance.

Of course, the movie theatre IS dark though…

The usual Generals, Colonels and soldiers appeared in a small skit depicting a scene of Navy men running off the ship in a foreign port of call. They had been relieved of their duties for a whole 24 hour vacation away from their service. The glee of the soldiers running down the gang plank gave all the youngsters in the audience the thrill of freedom just as if they were on that ship as well!

The next few scenes depicted the normal places young men in war might find in a foreign land, city street lights, pretty women on the streets and many bars.

During times of war it is a fact that life can be horrible to witness with the required fighting and ultimate death involved as well. Consequently, much of the soldier's 'rest and relaxation' was spent in search of liquor, cigarettes and women and a respite away from the horrors of war.

The movie showed some of these young men getting totally drunk on cheap liquor and being taken advantage of by 'ladies of the evening' and thugs. The skit showed the young men being so drunk they could not protect themselves and were relieved of their belongings and money.

The ultimate defeat was the young men losing all, even the means to get back to the ship. The intention of the Department of Defense was to force soldiers to keep their wits about them at all times and refrain from becoming fall-down-stinkin-drunk, thus falling into the clutches of criminals.

There were also strong verbal warnings (but no images) to protect themselves against sexually transmitted diseases. After all, this was long before the advent of X ratings for movies; therefore the censorship was high at best.

As the movie rolled, the general unrest of the audience was humming, the shuffling feet, the murmurs of young deep voices grew louder and the general disappointment was palpable within the theatre. Seats loudly popped into the upright position when youngsters became so dissatisfied they left the audience in sometimes loud fits of disgust.

Mutterings of 'total waste of time' were heard sporadically throughout the room.

During the showing of the movie, it became clear towards the end that this was NOT an explicit depiction of the act of procreation but was in fact a warning for the soldiers to keep their heads clear and alert when traveling in foreign ports.

The general consensus of the audience was however that they THOUGHT there would be more---maybe even pictures for gosh sakes!

The boys decided they had enough and maybe should just begin their trek back home. *Boy…what a waste of time*, they thought. The entire walk back home was a gripe session; they really thought they were going to learn something.

The fact of the matter was though that each could have probably taught the lessons much better since they were RAISED watching procreation via their own farm animals!

They all KNEW what to do; they just expected it might be made a little more concise; complete with pictures!

It was well after midnight when they arrived at the road to Charles Henry's home. Charles Henry parted company with G.W. to continue down the dirt trail east for the next mile to his home.

GW, however, had another three miles to trek alone in the total darkness. Once home he could not simply walk into the house and alert his Mother as to why he was so late coming in.

He chose instead to sneak in through the window, keeping as quiet as possible; he absolutely could NOT awaken the family. When they learned where he had been and why, there just might be repercussions he would rather not have to deal with.

His adrenalin and anxiety were extremely high and even though he had walked many miles both to town and then back home again, his nerves would not allow him to catch even as little as '40 winks' that night.

(The trip to this movie showing was a lesson they never shared with their parents and was only admitted by G.W. to this author when he was well into his eighties…)

The memory of that day was a sweet reminder of lost innocence, days gone by and expectations of youth.

(It also brought many chuckles to this author as well!)

The War – 1945

In late 1944 during World War II, Lois Annie's second husband, Clarence, Sr. was drafted into the military service and was immediately sent to the front to fight for our country.

Over the years of his son and step-daughter's growth, he had remained a farmer of the crops for most of their younger years. During the years of the War, an exemption was given to a farmer if he was the provider with children. He had been able to get an exemption from the draft for most of the years during the War due to his share cropping. However, the labor was very difficult and sometimes did not offer the funds necessary to keep a family of four growing and safe.

It became necessary in early 1944 to find a job at the local ice house and he was fortunate to remain in that position for a short time.

Unfortunately, since losing the draft exemption in the fall of 1944, he was drafted into the Military and sent for duty.

Lois Annie years later would relate she knew that cold and rainy Wednesday she would never see him return to her again. She felt it deep in her heart and her bones were "colder than I've ever felt" he would not survive. She stood in the cold and rain for the longest time at the train station rooted in her fear and depression of what she prayed would not happen.

Lois Annie, Lois Marion and Clarence, Jr. survived those terrible months in hardship but in hopes the terrible War would end soon and their husband and father would return home soon.

Lois Annie had gathered many scraps of cloth over the years and as her mother had taught, made good use of her time and energies. She used those scraps of cloth and made lovely quilts, each with a perfectly square piece of cloth sewn one to another. These quilts are referred to as *patchwork quilts* and many households used these lovely quilts made with pride by the residents for warmth on cold winter nights

Families even today treasure the ancient quilts in memory of those who have gone before and the hardships endured mean so much to so many.

The arrival of a telegram one day in 1945 notified the family their husband and father had been injured in a bombing in France; no further word of his progress or lack thereof was mentioned.

Lois Annie wrote at least one letter to her husband each day he had been apart from her; sometimes two or three to assure him he was missed back home. She also relayed community news to him as much as possible.

No further word was received from him over the course of the next weeks and months except from a nurse who had penned a letter dictated to her by Clarence, Sr. telling his family he was hospitalized but was okay.

Lois Annie continued those letters each evening by the light of the lamps. She hand-stitched the little squares of cloth for the next quilt to be completed in preparation for her husband's home-coming.

His letters had been few and far between but she had received no letters from him at all since early January of 1945. She also knew how difficult it was for a soldier to write when in the midst of war but kept her spirits as high as possible and prayed with her children daily for his safe return.

In her own letters to him she begged for his response to let her know how he was fairing.

The next package received by the family was a container of little blue Air Mail letters with very familiar hand writing on them, all tied up in a small bundle.

They excitedly began to open the bundle to see what these letters were but in horror soon realized the letters they had received were all HER OWN letters to her love and none had been unsealed.

All had been stamped, RETURN TO SENDER, DECEASED.

It was after receipt of this bundle they finally received the notification from the Department of War that Clarence, Sr. had in fact been killed on January 19, 1945 in France during the Battle of the Bulge and had already been entombed in a military cemetery in France. In fact the letter they received telling of his hospitalization and the letter from the nurse had been received months AFTER he had already passed away.

Lois Annie and her children were devastated. She had been dreaming of and writing about all manner of ways they could build a house of their own and wrote of those dreams and plans to him daily. They had together already purchased the property it was to be built upon in anticipation of his return.

Charles Henry heard of the horror of their news and went immediately to be with his lady love to help the newly widowed Lois Annie in any way his youth could offer.

He had grown to love his girlfriend's mother almost as much as the mother he had lost back in his early youth. He respected her as no other since he knew this was her second widowhood, all within her ages of twenty and thirty five.

He loved her as a person and always held her in utmost respect; he would be there for all of them. He vowed his respect and support to her from that day forward.

School Days in 'Town'

During the ensuing months of 1945, Lois Annie was able to find work in a local Lumber Company and the employees of that company were made aware of her predicament.

They grew to love her as much as her own family.

She likewise, proved to be a very savvy business woman in a world of men.

She earned their respect and admiration by her ability to interact with as much knowledge in the construction business as many men. The construction vendors grew to trust her knowledge and information as well. Her position was secretary and bookkeeper but her knowledge of materials was widely admired by her male peers.

She also had a deeper quest to accomplish the building of her own home for which the plot of land had already been purchased before she lost her husband to war. Her quest for knowledge took on an exceptionally important degree of urgency. She was determined to move her children into their own home so they would no longer live in share cropper or rented homes.

When the 'Widow's Pension' funds began coming from the US Government, she decided she must accomplish the building of the house of which she and Clarence, Sr. had dreamed.

Studying the art of building and materials and with the help of the professional employees within her company, she was fortunate to realize her dream. She was having a modest but very sturdy little two bedroom home on Hillsboro Street built for her little family. The house was only blocks from the local high school where Lois Marion and Clarence, Jr. attended classes.

Things were beginning to look up for the little family and Lois Annie treasured the relationship blossoming between her daughter and her 'young man' Charles Henry. He had proven himself to be extremely willing to help in things he could do to repair or build and took Clarence, Jr. under his own youthful wings to help give him a sense of an older male role model.

After all, he had been caretaker of his little sister, Juanita since her birth and would be glad to share his knowledge and himself with Lois Marion's little fatherless brother as well.

There was nothing Charles Henry would not try to do and most times he accomplished projects efficiently and completely. Only rarely were there things he would not be able to finish on his own.

Those things he would seek help from other individuals but would assure the completion at all costs.

The young couple's relationship was blossoming as they continued an exclusive relationship to one another. They were both very young and still in high school but the future looked bright for each.

Charles Henry was excelling in his job with the school, his studies, his FFA duties and helping his own little family succeed with their toils on the share cropper's farm.

Lois Marion was a popular but shy young girl in her local high school and was known as "the girl with the white shoes" by many of her classmates.

This moniker given her was a source of pride to her cleanliness and neatness and she never wanted to make anyone change their minds about her attendance to her own person. She became a very accomplished seamstress as Lois Annie had made both of her children learn to repair clothing at a young age. They used all manner of cloth for whatever needs they may have at any given time. Nothing was thrown away; everything found a use in some manner or another.

This was witnessed in the now put away memory quilt which held its revered place in Lois Annie's little home.

Lois Annie was extremely proud of her daughter's abilities with the sewing machine and encouraged her to learn all manner of sewing since there may be a future need. She hoped Lois Marion and Charles Henry would be able to make a life and a home together. Besides, Lois Anne secretly counted on the couple once wed having many little girls which would be dressed in her daughter's hand-created little dresses.

She dreamed of grandchildren and hoped there would be many in her future, both for her daughter and for her son as well some day.

She worked hard to make a new life for her children yet again without a husband and father-figure for her children.

The Break-up

By the year 1947 the young couple had been sending those treasured letters back and forth every week and the young man with the beautiful green eyes was traveling to see his new love as often as possible.

There came a time that year however when he would wonder if he was doing the right thing in pursuing a relationship at so young an age. He was all of sixteen years old.

In reality it was true that even in that time in history marriages were made very young and were totally accepted. The war was now over, life was beginning anew and he had a vision of a future. He wasn't sure he could make that happen if he were to start a new life with a wife.

She was a young girl in love and never saw it coming…a break-up.

One Tuesday in March the mail arrived and she anxiously opened the anticipated letter from her young man. With horror she realized he intended to break their relationship off! She had to read it over and over again before it finally sank in that he was telling her "good bye."

He began by apologizing and with as much devotion and care as possible attempted to lay out his reasoning in what he felt was an extremely important time in their lives.

"I am sorry to say I think we need to slow things down a little; it just seems we are going a little too fast. I think I'm too young to be so serious with one person and we just need to be apart for a little while. I have to admit to you I told a fib when we first met. I told you I was fifteen when I was really thirteen. I didn't feel you would be interested if you knew my true age. We are just too young to be this serious.

Let's just be pals. If I ask you for a date again later, would you accept?" He continued.

Her heart fell to her toes and with much heartache and sorrow she had to accept his decision. It was not an easy decision to make but she would not be one of those young girls who would go crying to him to try to change his mind.

In her resolve she decided however that she would not allow him to know the hurt he had heaped upon her. She would suffer in silence…

She would have to accept his decision and hope she could actually survive her life until the time he returned to her, if ever. She cried inconsolably.

Lois Annie was furious with the young man for hurting her daughter. Lois Marion went about her days like a 'zombie' for months thereafter and accomplished her daily life in a vacuum.

The young girl also resolved until such time as he changed his mind, she would have to continue on with her life. If there were other young men who wanted to take her out, she would definitely take them up on their offers!

She would not allow him or any others to recognize her heartache. She was determined to at least give a good performance her young love's decision had not affected her as deeply as it had. After all, in her mind she kept repeating *"He's not the ONLY fish in the sea!"*

Any and all offers for dates would be welcome but she would NOT become involved with any one for any serious relationship. There were many young men who were interested and with whom she accepted the offer of a date but at the end of each date she would be found crying inconsolably in her room.

No one ever fit the bill; she would never get over the loss of the love of her life!

For the next four months she would always be on the lookout to check for his presence in town on Saturdays.

In those days Saturdays were usually the day of visitation for the community, bringing most residents a day of fellowship with their neighbors. Those from the rural areas would drive to the main 'town' of the community and every parking space on the thoroughfare would contain an automobile of neighbors looking for a social meeting. Townspeople would walk to the downtown square to visit as well.

She was always on the lookout to catch even a glimpse of her love.

She saw him only one time during those four months. She was in the car with her Aunt Edith and Uncle Flake and caught a glimpse of him walking down the sidewalk. It did not appear he saw her.

The rest of that afternoon was spent crying her eyes out and brought all her pain back to the forefront once more. She was miserable!

On one occasion upon the arrival to her home, Uncle Flake yet again found her slumped over the chair in her home with runny nose and red rimmed tear filled eyes. His heart was broken to see his young niece whom he loved so dearly in total misery.

He gently whispered to her "You know if he IS the right one, if it's meant to be, it will happen!"

She appreciated his kindness and tenderness but it couldn't change the reality of the situation so the tears continued falling.

Four months after the initial break-up letter they would meet once more at the wedding reception of her step-cousin, Lula Mae and new husband, Kenneth who was also Charles Henry's very good friend from school.

The day was festive and brought the residents of the community where Charles Henry and Lois Marion had initially met at the wood sawin' years previous.

During the reception, she felt a tender touch to her shoulder and when she turned realized it was her love, her green eyed boy from the country, and the cause of her extreme heartache as well.

He cautiously and gently asked her "Hi there, how are you doing?"

With an uplifted but cautious heart she replied "Well, I'm doing just fine, thank you!"

No other conversation was made, it was somewhat cold on her part but deep down inside she was screaming *Why, oh why did you leave me?* The meeting was awkward on his part as well.

She did have her own pride however and didn't feel it an appropriate time or place to try to find out exactly why he felt he needed to break up their relationship in the first place.

The day ended and yet again she was inconsolable.

The following Tuesday brought one of the most treasured of all her letters. It was an 'I'm sorry' letter and she would keep it in memory of a most heartbroken yet a most glorious time in her entire life as well.

From his own hand:

March 17, 1947
Dear Marion:

How are you getting along this breezy night? As for me, I have worked pretty hard all day. Marion, I may as well get to the point. It may seem strange getting a letter from me again. You told me when we broke up that if I would ask you we could have another date together and that we would always be pals. But <u>darn</u>, that chum stuff! We can be happy lovers just as good as being helpless chums. The day of Lula Mae and Kenneth's marriage I realized then that I loved you more than I ever thought I had loved you. I tried to think that it was just child's love because you were the first one I had ever fallen in love with but now I realize that I was wrong.

The reason I wanted to break up is that I had lied to you about my age and I thought that made a heck of a difference but it don't. Another reason is because I thought I would grow tired of you soon after we were married but Marion I have gumption enough now to know that I'll never grow tired of you or that I ever expect to quit loving you because, Marion, my love is truer and greater deep down than you or I ever realized. I hope this letter is not too late for darling I love you terribly. More than I can tell you so if you'll only be mine once more and let me be yours forever I will be happy.

Marion, I know your love was greater than mine and I know it is not all gone. Somewhere along the line you love me, I hope. Maybe not as much as before but for our sake can't we try it over and forget certain parts of the past? I'm not just asking or telling you this but Marion, I'm begging for you with a love that is greater than ever before because now I know how much you are a part of me.

I must close with these four small words but they mean all the world to me, I'll always love you.

Charles
Answer soon about the date if you believe this letter; Saturday week---you set the time.
Love again.
If I'm tearing up something let me know and I'll understand. Maybe.
Consider yourself before doing anything.

Her heart soared and of course she would go on this date with him! She now had the difficult task of replying back to him accepting that date but telling him how much he had hurt her as well.

The actual letter written by Lois Marion has been forever lost. However, a first draft of her answer was saved but never sent and was preserved with her treasured letters from her love:

March 20, 1947
Dear Charles:

I received your nice letter today and indeed I was surprised. I hadn't seen you in a coon's age until Saturday. Where in the world have you been keeping yourself? I thought maybe I would see you sometime and talk to you a little. You know, even Chums talk to each other.

Yes, you are right about that chum stuff, there is no fun in it. You look like you have grown a lot taller than the last time I saw you. You looked swell.

Are you sure that your love is a true and a great love that belongs to only one girl in this lonely world? Are you sure it is I whom you love?

I guess you know you hurt the one who worshipped the very ground you walked on. It hurt deeply Charles, so deep that I couldn't even get my mind on my studies. To think I had loved you and trusted you for two long wonderful years and then you turned me down like I was just another girl in your life that didn't matter at all. Although I have been going out with boys, my life is still lonely. There is no doubt about it; I have had some wonderful times with them.

You remember I told you I wouldn't settle down with one for a long time? Well, so far, I have stuck to that. Jimmy told me once you wanted to make up with me but I didn't believe it and anyway, I didn't like this business of me telling him to tell you. That's too much like the courtship of Miles Standish, you remember? "Why don't you speak for yourself?"

She would accept his request but she also determined she would make him sweat a little for the pain he had caused her <u>first</u>!

Queen for a Day

Lois Marion's Home Economics teacher who was also a close neighbor to the family noticed the shy and retiring young beauty and recognized her talent with a sewing machine early on.

One of the class projects one year was for each girl to complete a project of some type of clothing. Lois Marion was the only one who chose wool with which to construct a suit. The young girl's choice of wool material was pinstripes and demanded exact alignment of those stripes.

She was determined it was going to be a masterpiece and knew she had found a talent in her own seamstress abilities. The completed project was to perfection and the young girl wore it with pride. The suit won her an award in her Home Economics class and helped Lois Marion gain a new confidante in her favorite teacher as well. She totally respected this woman and all her classmates loved the teacher just as much as she did.

Each year the PTA of her school held some sort of fund raising project. In October of 1947 they decided on a carnival in which there would be a beauty contest. Many young girls were asked to participate in the beauty contest but of the approximately twelve or so youngsters asked, there were only a few takers.

Lois Marion certainly did not want to be asked to participate in this and she would NOT volunteer to stand in front of others. She was entirely too shy to walk across a stage in front of her peers.

Her teacher may have been instrumental in volunteering her services due to the excellent work she had done but no one can remember exactly.

Somehow Lois Marion was talked into participating in this event and her friends became her assigned political advisors. The event was run somewhat as a political campaign and friends, Betty June, Grace and Jule were her managers.

Her political managers were to ask individuals to donate one penny toward the charity which would equate to one vote for her to win Halloween Queen of 1947 at the local High School. She decided this would not be too difficult and felt she wouldn't get enough votes to win anything anyway so why not? She didn't consider herself beautiful enough to be a Queen but thought it might be fun at any rate.

She would do her best.

The fund raising event was published throughout their little town and the townspeople were asked to give one penny per vote to their choice of Queen.

Her friends appeared to have been active in their political duties and when the deadline arrived and all monies were counted, she learned much to her pleasure but dismay as well that she had WON the treasured Queen of Halloween for the year of 1947.

Her total count of pennies equaled more than $57.00 from the small community which did not include any votes at all from her young boyfriend. She had not even told him of the fund raiser at all! This was quite a large amount of money in those days to be raised by one small, shy young lady.

The next runner up had raised somewhere in the neighborhood of $35.00 which proved a tidy sum for the charity, especially in the day's economics.

Lois Marion was honored with a cardboard golden crown, all her classmates congratulated her on the win, she had her picture taken in a lovely gown and the day was totally wonderful; a day to treasure.

Charles Henry was a proud young man indeed in the knowledge his young girlfriend was chosen as Queen. Since their previous 'break up' and their making up, he already had set her up as his own Queen in his young mind.

To him though, if others felt she was queen material, he was certainly proud to be holding her arm!

The Beauty Contest

March 13, 1948; daughter, Lois Marion, and mother, Lois Annie prepare to travel to Fernandina, Florida to attend the Festival of Flowers Beauty Contest. Lois Marion has been chosen to represent Lake City in the annual beauty contest held in the 20-acre *Gerbing's Gardens* sponsored by the Kiwanis.

The plot of land contains a 5 acre sunken garden of thousands of azaleas, camellias, roses and natural flora and fauna and is a living testament to the man, Gustav Gerbing and his love of nature. The venue is greatly revered by the Fernandina residents as a showplace of beautiful plants, fountains and walking trails located near the shores of the Amelia River.

Gustav George Gerbing is the owner of the gardens and has been laboring for years to build new varieties and stocks of the Camellia. A book entitled *Camellia* was published by Mr. Gerbing in 1943 and is the first book to illustrate camellias in color and life-size images.

He graciously offered his beautiful gardens to host the annual contest and festival of the day.

The month of March in Florida brings many beautiful blooms and wonders of nature. These celebrations and festivals are a welcome respite from the horrors of the war years. The communities needed to witness the renewal of their environment in the wonders and beauties of their gardens and surroundings. They greatly rejoiced when this time of year approached.

The beauty contests were greatly anticipated since it would usher the young beauties' participation in their own rites of passage into young ladies. Fortunately for everyone, the War was now over, life could begin anew and the communities could once again become normal and thriving.

The general consensus of the communities was "let's just get on with life and have some fun now!"

Representatives of the local Kiwanis, Lions, Rotary International, as well as the President of the University of Florida and the Mayor of Jacksonville, Florida are all officiating in the Beauty Contest in this year's Festival of Flowers and Lois Marion is a bundle of nerves.

In Fernandina Beach, the month of March has produced record downfalls of rain but the contest and festivities will go on as best they can, come rain or shine. The Lee High School band will be giving a concert in the beautiful gardens Sunday at 2:00 PM, with a parade of contestants for the Azalea Queen Crown continuing at 3:00 PM. The beauty contest follows and the contestants anxiously await the outcome of the afternoon.

Which lovely young lady will be crowned the Queen for 1948 in these lovely gardens?

Lois Marion, a very shy beauty from a small community southwest of Fernandina is honored to have been chosen for competition in the contest. Cousins Mabel and Rosalie were instrumental in helping their first cousin's daughter become a contestant and are convinced she will have a wonderful opportunity to shine in the contest.

Lois Annie, her daughter Lois Marion and son Clarence, Jr. are desperately in need of something exciting and positive in their lives. She is greatly honored and proud for her daughter to compete.

All eyes are on the prize but if it's not 'in the cards' for Lois Marion to win the contest, the ultimate experience of the race is all that matters. She will forever be able to say "I competed in a beauty contest once!"

The manner of the young seventeen year old is shy but quietly respectful and graceful. Her creamy white and clear complexion and lovely coal black long, wavy hair, complements of her deceased biological father, are greatly admired. Her father unfortunately had passed this life of a terminal illness when Lois Marion was only three weeks old, never even having known his daughter's gender.

This day brings a sad reminder of the loss of his witness to his daughter's life and is quietly and reverently noted by Lois Annie, her mother.

Lois Annie has suffered the loss of two husbands in her young life. Her daughter and son by her second husband became her greatest achievements and source of pride for the mild mannered young mother.

The little group prepares for the most wonderful day of young Lois Marion's life to date. Mother and Daughter are being chauffeured by Mr. and Mrs. Douglas, local members of the community who have the cherished good luck of owning a vehicle. They were kind enough to offer to drive mother and daughter the long miles east for the weekend festivities.

Lois Marion's steady boyfriend and soon to be husband, Charles Henry and Clarence, Jr., her only sibling and three years younger, are riding over from their hometown of Lake City with two cousins, Mabel and sister, Rosalie to witness the exciting competition.

Charles Henry is exceptionally proud his 'baby doll' is competing in this contest and must be there to witness the festivities, trusty camera in hand.

He was just barely dry behind the ears himself!

Mother and daughter arrive at the festivities and find there are 26 other young beauties competing on that day, including a set of twins. They had the good fortune to be able to spend a night in a real hotel, one Seaside Inn right on the ocean.

Lois Marion has not had much experience on the oceanfront so the stay in the hotel is quite a treat.

The Saturday practice event found the girls practicing their walks and turns on the very high stage set in the middle of the beautiful gardens. Each young lady was told to walk across the stage, turn then walk back across the stage. "And for goodness sakes, SMILE" one of the mothers instructed.

During their practice, the group of contestants was pleased to find an adjacent playground near the stage where picnic tables and swings were provided for children. Lois Marion and most of the young girls took turns swinging in those children's swings just as if they were still joyous children themselves. (They WERE still children!)

The evening festivities brought a wonderful meal in the banquet room of the Seaside Inn on the beach where contestants and chaperones were privileged to stay in a hotel room in preparation for the big day on Sunday.

Each young lady was assigned a young man to escort her to the evening event and would seat each in her respective place for the meal. The event was enjoyed by all and at the end of the evening each young lady would retire to her room to try to rest before her big day on Sunday.

Most would probably not succeed in restful slumber; most certainly not Lois Marion.

Fear and nerves arise for everyone; but most especially for this quiet and retiring young beauty. She has no idea if she can pull this one off.

"How in the world am I going to walk across that stage and let people look at me? I just know I'm going to make a fool of myself!" she said to her elders.

Last year she had been chosen Halloween Queen in her small hometown but this event was much bigger. It encompassed participants from all of Florida and part of Georgia as well.

She still could not believe she was chosen from her school to participate.

She had been called to the Principal's office one day and feared she had done something wrong. Instead she was told she had been nominated by 'someone' to participate in this large event. She had no earthly idea who had nominated her.

She absolutely could not turn down the experience but also suffered with a healthy set of nerves as well!

Cousin Mabel proclaims "Oh, do you think you're the ONLY one who is nervous here? Just think about how each and every one of those other 26 girls must feel; they're just as nervous and fearful of tripping or doing something wrong on that stage as you are. You have just as much beauty, grace and intelligence as any one of those beauties out there and don't you forget it either, young lady! We will all be in the audience cheering and loving you along each step you take" mother Lois Annie quietly reassures her young daughter.

Placing her kind and gentle hands on both of her daughter's cheeks and looking earnestly and confidently into her eyes she says "You just say a little prayer and do the very best you can; that's all that matters here. There is no reason for you to think we would be any less proud of you if you didn't win. You know, the Bible says don't hide your candle under a bushel" her mother gently admonishes. "I firmly believe that you can step up, be proud of who you are and keep your head held high. Go out there and show the audience what a proud and graceful young lady you are! We will be proud of you, win or lose!" exclaims Lois Annie with a smile and a hug for her daughter.

The band gave a wonderful concert, the parade was a great success and the day proceeded with much excitement. Lois Marion was called as the 25th contestant; that fact having made her nerves raw with expectation as she watched each successive young beauty cross that stage. As each contestant crossed, she felt the interminable time and worried more and more she would embarrass herself or her family.

However, her mother HAD told her she could do this and she knew Lois Annie would be proud of her attempts. She had strong convictions she would see it through. Besides, her young love was watching and she desired to make him proud as well.

When the time came for her to walk across the stage, take a few turns showing her lovely black frock and her beautiful smile, she felt more and more comfortable even though she was still fearful people might hear her knees knocking beneath her elegant dress. She truly felt like a princess.

(Years later she would laughingly admit "I was so nervous, I'm not even sure I smiled!")

After all 27 contestants had taken their first turns on the stage, the Judges made their decision and, wonder of all wonders; SHE was in the top six contestants. Her spirits soared and she stored up her confidence. She determined she would make her little audience proud; she would do the very best she could!

Charles Henry, trusty little camera in hand, was taking pictures of his 'baby doll' from the audience and could only point his camera high above the heads of the audience in front of him.

He meant to capture the moments of his love walking to the front of the stage then retreating. He could only pray he got her in the frame sufficiently

As the final six crossed the stage and the time came for the Judges' decisions, all of their collective nerves and excitement filled the stage. When the final name was called, "Jean Stafford of Palatka" the cheers went up and the audience went wild.

The remaining five contestants in the final judging were surely disappointed but Lois Marion was disappointed only momentarily; her way was not to be jealous of the other who had won the crown.

Lois Marion's only thought was *I did it and I did my family and Charles proud. That's all that matters. I can finally say I accomplished something but I'm mighty glad it's over!*

She set about asking all the contestants and Judges as well as Mr. Gerbing, the owner of those lovely gardens to autograph her treasured pamphlet of the event.

The completion of the contest was an excitement, a truly wonderful experience and she would not have changed one moment.

She retained those mementoes of this wonderful day in memory of a glorious and exciting experience.

Lois Marion on the day of the Beauty Contest in 1948

The 'Pig'

Lois Marion had a close cousin, Myrtice, who was just a few years older and daughter of her mother's cousin Mabel. Myrtice was always looked up to and admired by the shy and retiring young teenager. She felt Myrtice was so much more worldly and knowledgeable than she and loved to visit their homestead on Myrtice Road.

The homestead was a very stately old home encircled by a huge grove of mature lovely old oak trees with shadowy and billowing Spanish moss hanging from every branch of those beautiful old trees. There were extremely plentiful mature azalea and camellia bushes as well. It was a beautiful sight when those plants chose to show their lovely colorful pink blossoms.

At certain times of the year the property would be a sea of color rivaling even *Cypress Gardens*, a local tourist attraction and a 2 hour drive from their home town. The gardens featured water skiing shows, boat rides through the beautiful manicured gardens and graceful water fowl.

The attraction was most certainly a national treasure of the day.

When viewing the old homestead you almost expected to see lovely young beauties dressed in civil war period hoop skirts the old *Cypress Gardens* postcards of the time portrayed. It was every young girl's dream in those days to be one of those models seated on the beautiful grounds in front of a huge array of flowering plants in full splendor.

The home had been built by Myrtice's grandfather; the lumber having been hand-hewn from the timber felled on the same land. It was a grand old home and held many wonderful memories of generations of childhoods. The place held Lois Marion's imagination captive since her own homes had been much more humble than this lovely old home.

The girls had shared much of their earlier lives together when the occasions would allow and both looked forward to the company of the other for any and all reasons.

On one such occasion, in the days of Charles Henry's and Lois Marion's courting, Myrtice had possession of her father's old Plymouth vehicle and invited the young couple to go on a double-date.

Lois Marion was thrilled to be invited to participate with her young boyfriend so she couldn't wait to share her news with him. He lived not more than five miles farther from the old homestead on the same road but a letter would be required informing him of their wonderful opportunity to go with Myrtice and her boyfriend, Linwood.

The US Postal Service was a wondrous thing in those days. There were no telephones to allow them easy access to each other so they were content to continue their letter-writing.

Each Tuesday brought the treasured letters one to the other.

On the first day she was able to send him a letter informing him of the possibility of a date she excitedly outlined the prospect of double-dating with Linwood and Myrtice and asked if he would like to go.

"Of course, I'd love to go" was his immediate post. His family had no car and neither he nor Lois Marion had a driver's license in the first place.

This would be a lark!

The time was arranged, the young couples made the necessary meetings and they finally were on their own without the uncomfortable adult supervision; only another teenaged couple!

Since the car was owned by Myrtice's father, she was the one to drive but Charles Henry and Lois Marion were able to sit together on the back seat of that old Plymouth and enjoy the ride.

"Where're we going?" Charles Henry piped up.

"Well, we're going to go down to the Magnolia Drive-in" Linwood said.

The younger couple had not had much experience with going out to a restaurant and knew of the local drive-in called the *Magnolia* but neither had experienced it. Some of the more privileged kids in town who had access to vehicles viewed it as a local hangout of sorts in those days and it was quite popular.

The car-hop arrived at their window and Linwood leaned over Myrtice in the driver seat to make the order for the two of them.

Apparently the two older teenagers knew what to order and waved away the printed menu, assuming that the two younger teenagers already knew what they would order as well.

"Pig and a *Coke*; two please" he told her.

Myrtice and Linwood's assumptions that the younger couple had experienced this restaurant were sadly incorrect.

The youngsters in the back seat were both totally silent. Neither had any idea what a *Pig* and a *Coke* was!

The younger couple silently questioned, *what in the world is a 'Pig' and how are we going to order something when we don't even know what we're ordering?*

Neither would voice their questions openly; they couldn't appear to be country bumpkins by asking what might be a stupid question.

Charles Henry, being the young man and having the right manners to order for his girlfriend took the reins. Mustering as much confidence as possible, he answered the car-hop's query "We'll have the same please... two."

He silently prayed he would have enough money to pay for the treats but would not dare ask the question. After all, in those days it was the boy's obligation to pay for his date's pleasure.

Besides, that's just the way Charles Henry rolled. In his own simple way, he was just as much a knight on a shining white horse to Lois Marion as any fairy tale character.

At least to her way of thinking he was!

The car-hop took their orders, retreating into her assigned work area and gave their orders to the cook.

Charles Henry and Lois Marion worried silently, looking to each other with quizzical glances, *what in the world are they going to bring us?*

The young country boy guessed it must be something made of pork but had no earthly idea what it might be. They must not, however, appear ignorant or backward. Lois Marion's mind was running rampant trying to figure out what it might be as well but was too shy and timid to ask the question.

She didn't think Myrtice would steer her wrong; *still...*

Between the two of them, they only hoped they would not be too surprised by what would be delivered to them. Whatever it would be however, they both silently vowed to eat it completely but act as if they enjoyed it fully!

Suddenly Lois Marion thought *I only hope it's not so bad I gag when I taste it!*

She worried her face must be blushing bright red but could only pray none of the occupants of the car would notice.

The talk continued with the usual friendly joking and teasing between the two young men. The girls joined in when possible; Lois Marion remaining the most timid. They spent the next few minutes in camaraderie and pleasant talk; neither of the youngsters in the back seat querying the older couple as to exactly what they had ordered.

The car-hop arrived with their meal placed upon a cute little stainless steel serving tray with attached feet which she skillfully installed in the open window of Myrtice's car.

There were 4 drink glasses with what they knew would be the treasured drink of the day, *Coca Cola*. Of that they were mightily sure they could drink. However, they still didn't know what in the world the wrapped food would contain.

Myrtice handed the two paper-wrapped items; each with a toothpick inserted into the top of the paper to the youngsters in the back seat. The *Cokes* were handed back as well.

"ENJOY!" Myrtice shouted and she and Linwood proceeded to un-wrap their treasures, savoring the bites as if they just couldn't wait to get into those delights soon enough.

The time has arrived! Charles Henry carefully removed the toothpick and found a slice of dill pickle attached to the underside of the paper and top of the bun. Hoping he wouldn't be noticed, he quickly lifted one side of the bun to reveal the contents of the sandwich.

Lois Marion, following his lead, looked over at him with a slight questioning glance and did the same.

They each took their first very cautious bite and realized the bun contained a shredded meat which was extremely dense, well packed and piled high, a wonderful glaze of a sugary thick and sweet dark tomato sauce cooked into the meat. The meat was so tender it literally melted in their mouths!

Their amazement at the luscious flavor and culinary wonder of this new texture produced much relief and enjoyment to the taste buds!

Charles Henry, thoroughly enjoying his first bite of a new type of sandwich exclaimed "This is absolutely the best 'pig' I've ever tasted! How about you, Marion, don't you think it's just the best?"

So thoroughly was she enjoying every morsel, she could only shake her head in relief and affirmation of a glorious new taste! Greatly savoring the flavors of that first taste of a 'pig' they drew their new experience out just as long as they possibly could. Combining the flavor of the sugary, fizzy drink of *Coca Cola* with such a luscious treat in that barbequed pulled pork sandwich was such a wondrous new experience they vowed this would not be the LAST time they would partake of such a treat!

However, they vowed to never admit to her cousin and date that they actually HAD NO EARTHLY IDEA WHAT THEY WERE ORDERING!

They would remain as cool and worldly as the kids in the front seat but were also greatly relieved they had enjoyed their introduction to a new recipe for pork!

Senior Moments

During the following months the young couple courted when possible and each looked forward to the next letter. The days of school classes in different schools would cause the other to be unaware of each other's lives until that one shared with the other.

Some things would remain unshared for various reasons.

Charles Henry continued trying his best to get to his girlfriend's home each Saturday but life would periodically get in the way.

During the time in school, G.W. and Charles Henry were very good in their class studies and were each very active in the Future Farmers of America organization sponsored by their teacher. They were now seniors in high school and classes would soon be over for them!

Their teacher saw both young men as very talented in their fields and mentored them when possible. He had high hopes for their success and would help in any way possible.

One especially pleasant spring day during their senior year, the young men decided they just could NOT go to classes that day. Besides, school was going to be over in a few short weeks and what would it hurt to miss just one day of class?

They quietly planned an outing to the local springs for a day of swimming and just being teenagers. Ralph G., Charles Henry, G.W., and Ralph F decided they would find their way to these wonderful springs and take the heat if anyone caught them playing hooky from school.

They really thought no one would mind since they had been mostly good during the previous twelve years of school. Besides, the seniors of any given class SHOULD be a little special; at least that was their reasoning.

The waters of the springs are natural and feature crystal clear blue 72 degree year round temperature and those lovely springs were just calling to the boys. "**Come to me…come to me…COME TO ME!**"

The boys heeded the call and found their way to the head of the wonderful *Itchetucknee Springs*. These springs feature a boil which bubbles up millions of gallons of fresh clear cold water and were a natural draw to the residents of the community. The springs were found in the wilderness and truly were a sight to behold once one trekked through the brambles to get to it.

(In later years the property would be owned by the State of Florida and today boasts one of our most treasured summer locations as a State Park. A trip down this cold water river on an inner tube or a kayak is treasured by many in this location of North Central Florida.)

The boys found their way down to the springs, frolicked in the cool waters and left all manner of school studies, chores at home and worries about their futures behind.

When the time arrived for their return to school they attempted to blend back into the school day with hopes no one had noticed their absence.

Unfortunately in their young minds they did not take into account their treasured teacher would put two and two together and realize all four friends were missing at the same time.

With disappointment the teacher wondered. *Those boys HAD to be playing hooky from school but what kind of trouble did they get into while they were out?*

When the boys were grilled on their whereabouts they had to admit they had indeed skipped their classes and KNEW it wrong but the lovely day just made them all realize they needed a day to play. All were very remorseful for their actions but also knew they had to man-up and take their just punishments for their wrong-doing. After all, each had their own possible punishments when returning home. Their parents would certainly mete out discipline as well, senior or not!

The boys were sent to their beloved teacher who had supported them so well, mentoring them all so strongly and faithfully, but now each would have to guiltily admit his transgression.

The teacher read them the riot act and reacted much more angrily than any one of them had ever witnessed before. He left no doubt in their minds they had this time screwed up in a major way!

"What in the world do you think they will do to us?" they whispered to each other.

Charles Henry replied. "Well, surely it can't be that bad. It was just one day and we did come back, didn't we?"

With an angry expression their teacher fired out "You fellas did something today I NEVER thought I would live to see. I held each one of you up and would have fought for any one of you if needed. I trusted each of you and this act of defiance has disappointed not only your parents but you have killed any desire for me to help any one of you any more as well!"

As they stood facing the irate teacher, they worried at the ferocity of his words and realized the gravity of the situation. The red faces began to shine, knees began to tremble and perspiration fell like rain as they awaited their fates.

The teacher angrily but forcefully notified them "As you know, graduation is coming in just a few short weeks and we think each of you needs to be taught a very important lesson."

Each young man wanted to look to the other to see their reactions but didn't dare turn their attentions from the speaker…

The anticipation was just too much to bear!

Finally their teacher dropped the bomb.

"Each one of you will be allowed to walk with the rest of your classmates at Graduation but NONE of you will know if you have graduated. You won't know until I hand you your diploma! You just MAY have to repeat the twelfth grade!"

OH NO!

They would each have to walk across the stage and shake the hand of their beloved teacher, knowing of their transgressions and his disappointment with them. They would have to pass before their principal and all their classmates but would NOT know if they would have to repeat their twelfth grade until they unrolled that diploma!

The threat was made clear; that piece of paper just very well COULD be a blank piece of paper!

The next few weeks were extremely difficult for each of the boys.

G.W. had plans to attend college in the next city and plans would have to be put on hold until he could actually find out if he passed or not. Ralph G. had plans to enter the military at some point, but where would this setback land him if he didn't pass?

Charles Henry had plans to get a job since the thought of having the finances to enter college just was not in the cards for him. Besides, he and his girlfriend were getting pretty serious about their relationship lately. Was a job and marriage in the cards for him?

Ralph F. didn't worry too much; he would roll with the punches and see just where his luck landed him. He would laugh off the situation but deep inside there were doubts for him as well.

All four would fret silently however since the thought of having to go back through another year of high school just didn't appeal to any one of them.

The day of graduation came and nothing was said to the boys whether they would pass or not and as their teacher was a man of high integrity and most certainly a man of his word, he did NOT let on what the plans would be.

Each young man suffered in silence.

G.W. was elected as Valedictorian and Charles Henry was Salutatorian but they still knew there could be grave consequences on their skipped attendance. That fact remained a thorn in their sides all the way until the evening of the graduation ceremony.

Caps and gowns were fitted and lovingly regarded as a proud symbol of a task accomplished by most. For the young quartet, however, they knew there STILL could be a chance of failure.

The evening came, speeches were made and time arrived for diplomas to be awarded.

One by one the youngsters (all of 7 that year) walked across the stage to receive their white diploma; that symbol of the first real accomplishment for a school student.

The boys had devised a secret plan between them that when the first one walked, the very first thing he would do was peek inside that rolled up piece of white paper with the pretty gold ribbon to assure it was a REAL diploma and not just blank paper.

That one would raise his hand in triumph; a sign to the other three that the dreaded punishment was just a bluff! Ralph F. was the first to walk across the stage. As he walked, his footsteps were firm and strong but his knees were weak as he worried about the possible consequences of this walk.

He prayed his tube would be filled with his ticket to freedom, a real high school diploma!

Charles Henry, G.W. and Ralph G. all secretly prayed as they awaited their turns but were anxious to see just what Ralph F. had received. They reasoned if the first one got to graduate then they all would be safe after all!

After being handed the tube with the pretty gold ribbon tied around it, Ralph F. shook the hand of his principal then his beloved teacher and quickly peeked inside the tube...

"YES, YES ..." he shouted; his hand held high in triumph!

The audience laughed, never knowing the full ramifications of his action. They merely thought it was the youthful exuberance of a youngster proud to be relieved of his twelve-year obligation!

His steps became faster and lighter as he realized he was SAFE!

The other three remaining had been anxiously awaiting his reaction to the news and of course figured their fate would be exactly the same as the first since they all transgressed at the same time and in the same manner. Each with heads held high, their respective futures bright in their own minds, and absolute RELIEF flooding their souls now crossed that beautiful stage, accepted their REAL diplomas and shook the hand of their beloved teacher once more.

THEY HAD ALL FOUR BEEN SAVED!

Their teacher quietly watched the reactions of the youngsters knowing from the start he couldn't possibly fail these young men for so small an infraction. He had himself been young once and 'feeling his oats'; he couldn't really fault them for this one step out of line.

Besides they were all really good kids. He had taught them for so many years, watched them grow, loved them each and prayed for their safety and success in their respective futures.

His respect for those boys however would endure through many more years and the telling and retelling of the pleasure of seeing the boys sweat that night was an oft repeated and much treasured tale!

Wedding Day

A fter the young couple had both graduated from high school and spent five and a half years of steady courting, with one four month setback in 1947, Charles Henry and Lois Marion planned their wedding for January 9, 1949.

G.W. Charles Henry's boyhood friend was to be his best man.

Lois Marion had obtained a job with the local telephone company as a telephone operator fresh out of her senior year in high school. She was very pleased to have gotten the opportunity at such a young age and meant every penny she could scrap together would go toward their wedding in January.

She remained in her mother's new home and began planning for the big day. She faithfully paid the monthly rental of $15 to her mother for household expenses since she was now employed and was very proud to share in the costs of their home.

In those days, most especially after the War in this little part of the world, the luxury of a huge and costly formal affair on the most treasured day of a young girl's life was not usually afforded to most of the residents of their little community. However, it was also noted by the young couple they did not feel right expecting Lois Annie to pay for a formal affair.

The young couple planned to pay for as much as they could by themselves.

Lois Annie, however, knew in her own mind she would pay for either a rehearsal dinner or the reception held afterwards. She just couldn't afford to do both. The bride would pay for the wedding and was very proud to save her own hard-earned salary for their special day.

Charles Henry's contribution was the honeymoon and funds for which their first home together would need to be paid.

Their choice was to allow the bride's mother to put on the rehearsal dinner and they would forego a wedding reception entirely.

The usual tradition was for the groom's parents to pay for the rehearsal dinner but William Henry who was a widower himself with a young daughter still at home was in no financial position to put on much of a feast. Lois Annie's cousins, Mabel and Jessie volunteered to cook the meal and hosted the celebration at Jessie's home. The mother of the bride purchased all the food necessary for the feast. She was especially mindful however, to make the gift not appear as an act of charity. She knew William Henry was a very proud man.

Lois Annie made sure William Henry was included in the dinner and that he knew the cousins offered the rehearsal dinner thereby removing any obligation for his payment of the celebration.

The evening was a much enjoyed occasion by all and Mabel, who was a night clerk at the local Blanche Hotel was instrumental in helping the young couple receive a hotel room for their honeymoon night. The manager of the hotel had met young Lois Marion on her visits to her Aunt at the hotel and knew of the impending nuptials.

He very graciously offered the use of one of the rooms in the hotel as a wedding gift to the couple.

Charles Henry had never stayed in a hotel in all his life so the occasion was greatly appreciated. The young couple eagerly accepted the invitation.

The soon-to-be-bride had saved for her most special suit for her wedding and purchased her entire trousseau for the big day. Her lovely form fitting suit was perfectly suited to her lithe figure. Her shoes were carefully chosen and the beautiful corsage was a perfect and graceful orchid.

Lois Marion ordered a very large arrangement of white gladioli with many shades of green foliage in a standing urn for the focal point in the lovely sanctuary. The urn was placed in front of the position on which the young couple and the officiating pastor of the church would stand.

Charles Henry's boyhood friend, GW was attending him and her friend, Mona was attending as the Maid of Honor. Mona's young man, Marvin was also attending the young couple.

The young groom was fresh faced with green eyes dancing when he saw his intended walking down the aisle toward him escorted by her only sibling, Clarence, Jr.

Charles Henry felt himself a very lucky young man even if he was for all intents and purposes still 'wet behind the ears.' He had turned the ripe old age of eighteen the previous December and his intended had turned nineteen the previous October, a fact which would cause much teasing for her all the years of their marriage. Jokes of 'robbing the cradle' were told by many and most certainly by Charles Henry himself!

On the occasion of their first meeting, young Charles Henry had told a little fib about his true age knowing this new young lady was about to turn fifteen that month.

Instead of admitting his true age of thirteen, he told her he had turned fifteen in June of that year.

Earlier in their relationship as the youngsters became a 'couple', Lois Marion planned a party June 8 of the following year, and sent word to Juanita and her father there was to be a surprise birthday party she wanted them to attend. The party was enjoyed but Charles Henry had felt very guilty in his deceit for years.

Lois Marion would believe his falsified age until March 17 of 1947 when much to her sadness the couple actually broke up for an entire four months.

During a very beautiful letter sent to his girlfriend, Charles Henry spilled the beans of his falsehood and finally came clean.

She had decided through their courtship that their differences in age didn't really matter and knew in her heart he was her soul mate. He had already recognized the differences didn't matter as well.

On January 9, 1949 they joined hands at the church altar and together vowed to raise a happy home with lots of children!

He had told her many times in their young relationship <u>she</u> was the one he wanted as the mother of his children and that they would NEVER go hungry. He promised when they walked together, he would always hold her hand and upon each arrival and departure from their home he would share a kiss with her until his dying day.

Charles Henry had also gained employment after his graduating as Salutatorian of his little community school in 1948. He was surely glad to be getting on with his life and claiming his young bride.

The big day arrived and the young couple stood in that beautiful church which would become their life-long church home and repeated their vows… "Till death do us part."

The ceremony was beautiful and enjoyed by friends and family.

The youngsters prepared for their first night together and the start of a new life.

Lois Annie presented her daughter and new son-in-law with the total payments Lois Marion had been paying for her monthly rental in the family home. She had requested the $15 monthly from her daughter to begin teaching budgeting necessary for a household. She never intended to keep the funds however and the young couple was highly impressed she would offer its return.

During the course of the remainder of the afternoon however Mona and Marvin, the young friends who had just stood up for them in their wedding, found the newlywed couple and asked them to help in their own quest for marriage vows.

Mona and Marvin's parents did not see eye to eye with their children's choice of spouses and therefore did not give their consent for the marriage. Neither had graduated yet but Marvin was intent on having Mona as his bride.

Between the two they convinced the newlyweds to drive with them over the State Line that same day and stand in front of a Justice of the Peace to repeat their vows. There were no three-day waiting periods to be dealt with in the adjacent state so they determined they WOULD repeat their vows that same day if their friends would help.

The youngsters felt since they were so honored to have been helped by their friends in their own ceremony, the least they could do was to stand up for them in turn.

Mona and Marvin stood together in the same wedding attire as were Lois Marion and Charles Henry and now the Maid of Honor would be the bride and Lois Marion would be not be her MAID of Honor but now her MATRON of honor.

They determined they had done a good turn for their friends and wanted them to share in the joy of a new start in life if it was their express intent.

Besides, there would be a lifetime to share each other.

This one little act of kindness and sharing would be with them for the remainder of their days and the couples celebrated many anniversaries together during the following years.

January 9, 1949, newlyweds Lois Marion and Charles Henry Hines

Hal Henry #1

Late spring 1949 as Lois Marion and Charles Henry were beginning their young lives together she began to experience very unusual nausea and a general malaise.

Her young husband had no idea what was happening nor did Lois Marion suspect any change in their family might be occurring. They just knew they were madly in love with each other.

Years later she would relate "We were green as gourds and had no idea at all in the beginning!"

Their youth proved their total oblivion and naiveté to the natural order of the human experience and were not prepared to begin their new family so early in their young marriage. However, as nature would have it, Lois Marion would experience two months of extreme morning sickness and Charles Henry could only hold her hand and worry about what was happening. A trip to the family doctor confirmed they were indeed to become parents by the end of the year.

Charles Henry was determined to provide for his new little family as best he could.

Christmas of 1949 brought much happiness to the young couple.

During the Christmas celebration of that year with her mother's family and Charles Henry's family in attendance as well, they gathered for the traditional celebration of the birth of Christ.

Lois Marion had endured a normal pregnancy to this point and as her Grandmother Eva Marion had explained what to expect, awaited the coming birth. As a matter of fact, her Grandmother had birthed fifteen children to date and after the youngster's initial embarrassment was overcome, her Grandmother's experiences would be much sought after by the young bride.

On the day before Christmas she had been experiencing strange sensations and knew her time was coming very soon but felt she could safely attend the celebration. She prayed nature would stay the course until after the festivities were complete.

The extremely large family gathering was a hit that year and the young family attended the entire event.

The couple had been choosing names for their new addition to the family and Charles Henry was convinced his first child would be a boy. They decided to call him Hal Henry in honor of Charles Henry's father. If it was a girl, her name would be Dell Anne in honor of a Granny (Della, mother of Lois Marion's deceased biological father), a Grandmother, (Ola Dell, Charles Henry's mother who passed away in childbirth with his youngest sister Juanita) and Anne for Lois Marion's mother, (Lois Annie).

Both, however, only prayed for a healthy child, no matter what gender they were blessed to receive.

After what seemed to Lois Marion an eternity, at 5:01 AM on December 26, 1949, their first daughter, Dell Anne arrived.

The child flourished, was treasured by her new family and surviving Grandparents and life was good for Lois Marion and Charles Henry.

Trips to the country home of William Henry would be joy to Juanita who was enamored with the new baby and helped in any way she could. William Henry doted on the little girl and made a very crudely constructed high chair for those cherished meals in his humble little home. The first meals for the baby were very early and consisted of grits and eggs which would become favorite fare of the child later in life.

Family gatherings around his tiny little kitchen table in the crude shack in which William Henry and Juanita made their home were lively and the child became the center of attention.

She had a tendency to fall asleep very easily and William Henry laughed uncontrollably when her little head lolled to the side, eyes rolled up into her head and she would pitch forward right into the tiny plate of grits and eggs on the tray of her high chair.

Her little curly locks would be completely covered with grits and she would remain there…peacefully sleeping face down in her food. Many times even the jostling of being picked up and prepared for bed went un-noticed by the child as she slumbered effortlessly and comfortably.

Many such evenings were treasured by all.

The trips to see Granddaddy were few and far between sometimes with working, church attendance and just making a living but when the occasion arose, William Henry was "pleased as punch!"

As the child grew, William Henry would hike her upon his shoulders and walk down the dirt road to the little country store. He would allow her to put her chubby little toddler hands into the *Tom's Cookie* Jar with the great big red lid and choose her very own huge pink icing frosted oatmeal cookie.

(Heaven only knows what the store keeper might have thought of this practice…although William Henry would have taken care of any damages possibly occurring at his baby granddaughter's hands.)

Nothing was too good for his grandbaby.

She was not the first grandchild but Barbara, Mary and Junior, grandchildren by his oldest daughter Maude unfortunately lived far to the south and visits with them were even less frequent due to the distance involved.

Black and white pictures would have to suffice for his grandbaby 'fixes' for those three. This little one was the closest and he would shower as much love on her as he could share.

Since Lois Annie lived in the same town where her daughter, new husband and now new Granddaughter lived, the trips to see Grandmother were much more frequent.

As the first grandchild into Lois Annie's family and a little girl at that, there was no shortage of little dresses, toys and baby things to be had.

Great Grandmother Eva Marion was just as enamored of the new curly headed, black eyed little girl as her parents and grandparents.

Life was good for all…

A New Patriarch

In the summer of 1952 William Henry who had previously taken Charles Henry's custodial position with the old school after his son graduated from high school, was having many problems with his legs. Deep varicose veins caused him much suffering and there came a time when he could no longer stand for any reasonable amount of time.

During the time of his leg problems he became seriously ill with frequent headaches and suffered many days of hardship.

Unfortunately when he was finally able to visit a doctor the diagnosis was not good; he suffered from hardening of the arteries. The decision was made to do a very serious brain operation in an attempt to learn the extent of his illness.

The young son was very worried about the outcome. He knew however even though he was a working man and the hospital where his father would be operated on was sixty miles to the east, he would do all in his power to be at his father's bedside at every turn possible.

Juanita who was twelve years old at this time stayed with her father in the hospital in the unfamiliar town to the east of their home. It must have been very frightening for a small girl but had to be done nonetheless since neither Charles Henry nor his young wife could be there to help out.

The son would drive the long distance as often as possible to visit with his father before the surgery but would definitely be there the day of the surgery at his father's awakening.

The surgery was long, tedious and dangerous. The surgeon declared the problem was the cells of the brain were dying; being choked out by 'hardening of the arteries.'

His most disturbing symptoms which caused his visit for medical care was while walking down their dirt road to the store, he would start out in one rut but before getting to his destination he would be in the opposite rut and would have no memory of crossing over. It greatly disturbed him and he knew in his heart there was a major issue developing.

Brain surgery was performed to try to determine the cause of his disturbing symptoms. Unfortunately, the prognosis was not good for a long life.

Charles Henry stayed as long as he could on that day but had to return home to attend his work. After all, bills continued regardless of his family's condition and he was determined not to let anyone down.

William Henry improved for a while and Juanita, Charles Henry and sometimes Lois Marion would sit by his bedside in the hospital with him while his wounds were attended.

Juanita began longing for her own home but could not stay out in the country to attend her school classes all by herself so would be periodically given a rest and driven back home with Lois Marion. Those were very long and tiring days and nights during the recuperation.

When William Henry began making such improvement in his health that he no longer needed someone to sit with him, his family decided it would be okay for Charles Henry to focus on his job.

Lois Marion could focus on her job at the telephone company and her baby daughter, and Juanita could just be a child for a little while.

One day soon thereafter Charles Henry was on the job when his wife received a frantic phone call from the hospital. She had been told to get her husband to the hospital NOW, that there had been a change in his father's condition.

The change came up very suddenly as the day before it was evident the patient was on the mend and things looked much more rosy for his future. No one would know what the next few hours would hold and no one expected the worst. Unfortunately, the varicose veins and hardening of the arteries were working their damage...

By the time Charles Henry and Lois Marion arrived at the hospital, William Henry's hospital bed was remade and no sign of his beloved father was evident.

Frantically they went to the nurse's station and inquired of his condition.

The charge nurse asked "Didn't they tell you?"

With anticipation and dread the young man answered "No."

The nurse then gently informed them. "Mr. Hines expired this morning..."

To their horror they learned that when the telephone call had been made earlier to notify them, Charles Henry's father had already passed this life! The end was here and his beloved father, William Henry, his only surviving parent was deceased at the age of fifty-four years.

The son was now twenty one years of age and was to shoulder the entire load of young husband, father to a toddler, yet again care for his twelve year old sister, provide for the family and finally become Patriarch of his little family of two sisters.

He was also the oldest male of his young wife's clan which included her widowed mother and young brother. His plate was surely full but he asserted "I've got broad shoulders and I can handle it!" Those days were full of sorrow but also full of determination that Charles Henry would fulfill all his obligations of 'Patriarch' for this family and fulfill them with an abundance of loving care...

This tragedy would <u>not</u> taint his resolve, his courage or his devotion!

The House on Fifth Street

The young family had lived in rented apartments in the early years of their marriage and always planned to purchase a small starter home when the time was right.

Lois Annie had built her treasured home on Hillsboro Street and the neighborhood was lined with small wooden homes built in the thirties and forties. The lots were small with very mature oak trees shading the streets and were located near the local football and softball fields of the community.

The back of the neighborhood was lined with the local tobacco selling warehouses bordered by a railroad track. Just down the street there was a very well established park for tennis, picnic tables and children's playground equipment. There also was a local swimming pool located just across the street from the park.

In the fall of the year the softball field was the site of the local county fair and brought the carnival and joy rides to the area each year.

Behind the neighborhood the residents would be privy to the local football games on Friday nights and could hear the bands playing and cheers when touchdowns were made.

Lois Annie worked with Mr. Mac who lived just down the street. He knew the young couple was searching for their first home and told her of a little house fronting Fifth Street coming up for sale by his neighbor.

His neighbor owned two houses on the block and decided he did not want to be a landlord any longer. He decided the tenants would move and he would sell the little white wooden house. The couple had already seen the house and both fell absolutely in love with the looks of it. When they learned it was going to be for sale they jumped at the chance to look into the purchase.

As luck would have it, their dreams were quickly realized when the owner decided to sell to the young couple. The papers were signed, sealed and delivered and they set about moving into their new home.

Lois Marion and Charles Henry felt they had purchased the most beautiful home in the world; it was theirs (and the bank of course but MOSTLY theirs!)

The house was fully furnished and they set about placing their personal stamp upon it and made it their new family home. It boasted two bedrooms, a living room, a tiny kitchen and a breakfast room. It also had a very tiny unattached garage. There was a lovely screened-in front porch with shades around the entire porch to shade the structure from the heat of the days.

There was a fireplace and a kerosene heated furnace with the old fashioned grate in the hallway floor to heat the home. The kitchen had only two overhead wooden cabinets on either side of the cast iron sink and the stove was a monstrosity which took up half the room. The other half of the room contained the porcelain cabinet which housed Lois Marion's cooking pots and anything else she needed to store.

The breakfast room had an exit door to the back yard and the entire room had windows which let in lots of sunshine provided the oak trees didn't block the sun.

The one bathroom was roomy and had all the fixtures necessary for a family of three. They were pleased and proud to own that little house and began planning their futures in their new home.

The greatest thing of all was that it was within walking distance to Lois Annie's home.

Charles Henry was adamant that they not buy anything on credit except the house so they scrimped and saved for any new necessities to place in that little house and were mighty proud.

He had made a promise to his bride on their wedding day that upon each arrival or departure from their home he would share a sweet kiss with her and he was surely a man of his word.

Life was good in the little house on Fifth Street…

Horror on Fifth Street

The summer nights were hot and muggy in the little neighborhood on Fifth Street and all the Mamas, Papas and babies were sound asleep. Within each block there was a group of six homes, each with its own driveway and garage but very limited yard space within each plat of land.

Many of the homeowners were young middle class working families which brought many young children to the neighborhood and provided much activity during the daylight hours.

As for the nights, however, all slept quietly and soundly.

The neighboring high school football field was quiet and the adjacent tobacco barns were all tightly sealed. Even the railroad which ran behind the tobacco barns was totally silent. No sounds were heard save for the chirping of the crickets and the occasional barking of a neighboring family dog. Distant sounds of passing traffic on the main highway through town might be heard occasionally.

The heat was oppressive in that year and all the residents of the neighborhood slept with windows and doors wide open to catch any cool breezes.

Most homes in this little neighborhood did not boast air conditioning at the time and only a few might have fans to help ease the heat of the North Central Florida nights.

The street lights in front of the young couple's new house on Fifth Street shone their beacons of light across the smooth hardwood floors but afforded only a low and comforting light into the darkness.

Sleeping in the bed with their firstborn daughter, Dell Anne, Lois Marion was in the second bedroom of the small but comfortable home. The child was still prone to falling from the 'big girl bed' since she had very recently been removed from the infant crib. The young mother would stay with her daughter for a time during the night.

Charles Henry was sleeping in their marital bed but always had an 'ear open' for problems arising within his little family circle. Even though he was in his very early twenties, he was nonetheless cognizant of danger where his young wife and daughter were concerned.

He was fiercely protective of both.

The night was Friday and most assuredly he would be able to catch a few more 'z's tonight since he would not have to work his day job with the Power Company tomorrow.

70

He was, however, a young man from the country life and as such usually arose 'with the chickens' so to speak. His routine was usually that his 'feet began curling round the perch' when the sun went down.

Before the sun began to inch its way into the horizon, however he was usually to be found working at some chore or another well before the cock crowed.

He had worked for a minimalist pay but was proud to have received that well-earned paycheck at any rate. He had garnered this coveted job with the Power Company early on in their marriage and was proud to offer his skills and learn the trade of a power lineman.

His Friday afternoon had been spent on the way home by cashing his check at the local bank.

Most of their bills at the time were paid in hard cash and he was very proud to be able to do it. No credit for HIS family!

Those bi-weekly Friday afternoon paydays were much anticipated by the young couple since they were adamantly attentive to their budget and the necessary household bills.

Such was the case on this hot and muggy Friday evening.

Lois Marion had been dreamily sleeping; their daughter slept like the dead as well but suddenly the young wife awoke with a start and experienced an overpowering sense of a presence in the room. She knew she had been dreaming and had been quite soundly asleep but SHE FELT SOMETHING JUST WAS NOT RIGHT!

She felt more than saw something at first but lay perfectly still awaiting the arrival of her complete awakening before getting out of bed. As she lay in the bed with her little toddler at her side she felt a slight rustling to her right. She knew it was not her daughter because the toddler was to her left.

As she lay perfectly still in that little bed she thought. *Is it my imagination or is someone in this room with me?* She mused to herself as she lay alert and listening. *Of course*, she thinks, *what a 'scaredy-cat' I am…that's just Charles coming in to check on us…Why in the world do I let myself get so worked up over things? I'm not afraid of the dark and I don't have problems sleeping by myself. I do much prefer sleeping with him though!*

Feeling a little more relieved now she called her young husband's name "Charles…what's the matter, are you alright?" she asked.

No answer…

Again she called his name "Charles?"

Upon her second call she heard a muffled "yeah?"

Her immediate response was a fearful *THAT WAS <u>NOT</u> MY CHARLES!*

Her eyes flew open but her body remained completely paralyzed in fear.

With waves of extreme panic and fear she chastised herself. *I have to scream but I can't open my mouth…I can't even get myself up out of this bed! WHAT IN THE WORLD CAN I DO? I have to do SOMETHING but I'm not sure if I have the strength!*

The very small sliver of moonbeam on the shiny hardwood floor revealed a shoe; one which her husband would not have worn even if he had owned them. The intruder's dungaree pants legs were rolled up as was the habit of many young people of the day.

With extreme panic she realized THIS DEFINITELY WAS NOT HER HUSBAND!

The dark figure standing at the bureau in that little room was totally frozen, uttering no sound at all.

It appeared neither individual, the young woman in the bed, nor the intruder in the home could utter a sound; both had appeared to have stopped breathing entirely!

As Lois Marion continued to lay frozen with fear, the intruder very quietly and with much stealth began to inch his way back out of the bedroom. A possible thought inside the intruder's mind at the moment might have been *I'd better start 'pickin em up and putting em down' fast; get the heck out of this house before I really get into trouble!*

At that moment, the neighboring highway just a few blocks over brought the loud rumbling of a semi-tractor/trailer rig rolling down the street on its way through the sleepy little town.

Certain road sounds were many times loud but the neighbors had mostly grown used to sleeping through those noises overnight. Such was the case when Lois Marion finally gained enough courage to make a noise.

Just as the semi ran its course past the neighborhood and she knew the rumbling would not drown out her screams she gathered up all her strength, sat straight up in bed and began screaming at the top of her lungs!

With all the courage and breath she could muster and hopefully with all the VOLUME as well she screamed **"CCCCHHHAAAAA RRRRLLLLEEESSSSS!!!!! HHHHEEEEELLLLLLPPPPP!"**

She screamed and screamed and screamed until there was no longer any breath within her to scream any longer. Her tears fell like rain and all the lights in that little neighborhood came on with haste. Her husband who made a habit in the summer of sleeping 'buff' came running into the room with every hair standing straight up on end to see what his wife was screaming about.

He heard the sound of heavy footsteps but ran directly to the other bedroom where his little family slept. His young wife was in total meltdown!

Stammering profusely he asked "MARION...WHAT'S THE MATTER...ARE YOU ALRIGHT...WHAT THE DEVIL IS WRONG? IS THE BABY OKAY? WHAT IS IT?"

Hysterically alternately screaming then crying, she finally could answer him with "THERE'S SOMEBODY IN OUR HOUSE AND HE WAS STANDING OVER ME AND THE BABY...I THOUGHT IT WAS YOU BUT YOU WOULDN'T ANSWER. WHEN HE FINALLY DID SAY SOMETHING I KNEW IT WAS NOT YOU...OH, CHARLES, I'M TERRIFIED!"

She could hardly even talk to him she was trembling and crying so uncontrollably.

*OK, I have to get it together...*he said to himself. *I have to find out if this guy is still in the house and protect my family!*

After quickly assuring his family was alright, Charles ran back to the bedroom, hastily drew on his shorts and was running through the house searching for whoever had been in their home. As he was running and searching in that small house, he heard the screen door slam as someone ran down the back doorsteps and out into the yard.

The pounding of running footsteps on those floor boards now was causing quite a commotion! Charles Henry's adrenalin was pumping so hard he could hardly breathe but he had to get out there and try to catch whoever had been inside his castle!

There was no fence around the home at that time so anyone leaving could have easily run in any one of four directions. The street lights proved by fresh foot prints the intruder had crossed the street and jumped not one but two six foot board fences!

From there he had totally disappeared.

When Charles Henry had taken all directions and found no sign of the stranger he began to notice many of his neighbors had now been roused from their slumber as well and someone had phoned the local Police. They were already on their way!

The neighbors who arrived on the scene to help the young couple in their time of trouble began to piece together what had transpired.

When the Police arrived they began questioning the couple "Is there anything missing from your house?"

Charles Henry had not even begun to think of what valuables they might have lost but immediately searched the end table next to their couch where he usually left his wallet.

Unfortunately, those wondrous street lights had shone their bright lights right upon his trusty wallet with his entire fortune for two weeks of work!

The light beams simply danced on the shiny surface of the end table effectively marking the exact location of the valuables contained there.

Fortunately, however, his car keys were still in their usual place and safe.

His heart sank to his toes as his fear of the loss of two whole weeks of pay might mean to his family. To his horror he realized *MY WALLET IS NOT HERE!* His pay was missing and his next thought was *how in the world will we pay next week's bills?*

He couldn't allow his young wife to worry about that at the moment so he quietly told the Officer "Yes, there is something missing; my whole pay check, I just cashed it this afternoon!"

With further horror he realized his favored picture of his now deceased father was in that wallet and heaven only knows if he would ever see it again.

He was the treasurer of the Union at work and had two checks in his wallet that day. He worried about the repercussions of someone getting their hands on Union funds. Of course, that was luck however, since they were checks and he would have the banks stop the checks immediately; at least that was a blessing!

When Lois Marion heard of the loss, her tears and sorrow fell all over again. She knew how hard it was for them to pay their bills each week and also that her husband was too proud to ever accept charity from anyone so she fretted just how they were going to manage.

She likewise was too proud to ask for help from her widowed mother. Her mother did not make an overabundance of money herself and still needed to support Lois Marion's younger teenaged brother.

"What will we do, Charles?" she asked through her tears.

Fearing another meltdown by his beautiful young love he told her "Well, we can get through it honey so don't worry right now. Let's just let the Officer do his job and hopefully they can find the thief and get our money back."

Many men of the neighborhood arrived after having been alerted by that blood curdling scream and searched their own properties in hopes of catching the culprit.

The Officer had a very large spotlight and was able to show where the intruder had cut the rear screen door to gain entrance into the house.

They spotted the path taken by the intruder and that he had looked into the windows of both the houses; that of the young couple and also the next door neighbors, George and Betty. The cool dirt revealed footprints to which the Officer placed his own foot directly onto the top of the ONE good print in the sand.

With much importance he told the young men gathered there "Well, whoever he is…he wears a size nine shoe; just like mine!"

(He totally damaged the shoe print..!)

The neighborhood was searched as well as possible. There was no 'forensic evidence' to be had in that little sleepy town and in fact it didn't warrant searching for finger prints since there might possibly be nothing to compare prints with any way.

With reluctance the Officer told the young people gathered there "Well, folks, I guess there's nothing much more to do here tonight. Ya'll just need to go on back to bed, make sure you lock your doors and we'll look some more tomorrow."

The little group scattered back to their respective homes, checked on their children and in fact did make sure all their own doors got locked from then on …hot weather or not!

Unfortunately, the Police never caught that thief, their money was never returned and the Union check for dues was protected by the stop payment at the bank. Charles Henry was a little more open to sleeping in at least a pair of shorts and Lois Marion would never again sleep without her husband if she could help it…

The fact of the matter was however that Charles Henry WAS right in a few important facts:

1. Through the grace of God they survived to the next pay period without his paycheck and were thankful the paycheck was ALL they lost that night!
2. He learned their firstborn could sleep through a tornado!
3. His shy, demure and quietly retiring young wife had a set of lungs on her that just would not quit!

With green eyes sparkling and a mischievous chuckle he proudly wondered. *Where the devil did THAT come from?*

And Then There Were Four

The little house became lively with the addition of a young teenaged girl when Juanita and the pressures of growing into adulthood became a way of life for the young household.

With those pressures of a young teenager in the family unit, a young toddler, a very young wife who was quickly learning the pitfalls of motherhood and the young man who was responsible for feeding, clothing and offering a roof over all their heads, the household at times was not necessarily harmonious.

Young Juanita had never known her mother and the fact that now her father had passed away as well threw a pall over the family as she struggled to fit into her brother and sister-in-law's young family. She was just old enough to be a comfort and big sister to the toddler, Dell Anne, but just young enough to need corrections from the older adults at times.

William Henry, being a widower with Juanita as a newborn, did not necessarily offer her lessons in certain aspects of a maturing young lady. Lois Marion and Lois Annie both offered their personal lessons and values when possible.

Juanita attended her school classes and went to church services with her brother and new sister-in-law and became a treasured member of the family.

Nights of the two women of the household were many times spent at the kitchen sink talking and laughing with each other while washing and drying the dishes from the evening meal.

Lois Marion had taken it upon herself to learn more about cooking and did her best to keep a good meal on the family table. She had been given a beautiful hand-made, bound recipe book on the occasion of her marriage by her mother's cousin, Mabel. The young wife could be found many times pouring over those treasured recipes and deciding to test out yet one more recipe to please her man.

(Years later she would relate "I tried making homemade biscuits as good as Grandmother's but when I took them out of the oven and put them on the plate, had I dropped them on the floor, they were so hard, they would have broken right through the floor boards!")

Her tries at making those biscuits would not cease, however, and over a period of time she became very adept at making good biscuits. (She had plenty of practice over the years!)

There were nights of what one might consider a meager meal which might include white rice stirred into a glass of really cold fresh milk and biscuits with cane syrup. Other nights the family enjoyed "breakfast for supper" which would include homemade biscuits, fried eggs, grits and bacon and always the much loved cane syrup.

Lois Marion's Aunt Doris and Uncle E.V. had a farm north of town and each year made their own cane syrup. This syrup was a family favorite for years and the occasion to make it was a treasured tradition for many.

During the cool of the year when the sugar cane was ready for harvest, the families gathered the sweet canes and helped with the extremely tedious job of grinding then cooking the cane juice into dark sticky, very sweet syrup. The work might begin during the day but the evenings would be anticipated and enjoyed for the pleasure of the bonfires.

The children played all sorts of games, the adults and older children harvested the canes, cut it and with the help of the old mule produced this treasured sweet treat. The occasion was enjoyed by many families and most times involved a covered dish dinner where all enjoyed sharing the bounties of the fields.

The mule was tied to a pole and coaxed to walk round and round the old mill; each turn pressing the cane stalks deeper and deeper into the mill. The wondrous juice flowed from the spout which in turn was transferred to the cooker.

Uncle E.V. had a very treasured huge black cooker or caldron sitting atop a blazing fire which was tended by the adult men. The caldron had a lip around the edge that enabled sugar remnants to adhere to the surface once the juice began to boil and thicken. The ground cane juice boiled until the entire mixture became thick and dark. When the pot had been cooking for some time, everyone was excited to know exactly when it was ready for bottling.

"Is it pole cat yet?" the children would ask.

('Pole cat' when referring to cane syrup making is the process of cooking the juice down for hours until a thick sugary residue begins to form around the rim of the cooker or caldron. One might take a cutting of a cane stalk and drag it through the 'pole cat' for a sugary treat. The last 'cooking' might entail boiling the mixture until it becomes extremely thick and with buttered hands two individuals could pull and stretch the mixture until it became candy-like. This is somewhat similar to a treat known as taffy.

The build-up of sugar crystals left untouched for a while would become rock candy and at times if an especially large chunk of candy was left inside the syrup bottle, the bottle just might have to be sacrificed to retrieve those crystals within.)

Uncle E.V. with a wink might say "Nawww, it ain't ready yet but you'll be the FIRST to know when it is!" This was his standard answer to any and all so everyone knew they had better wait until he announced "Pole cat" then it was 'every man for himself' to get to the treat!

Uncle E.V. had a very dry wit and many would be left wondering when he was telling the truth or in fact kidding. You had to really be on your toes! Everyone knew he would tell ALL they would be notified first!

Charles Henry and Uncle E.V. would many times trade jokes and stories, leaving family and friends sore from laughter during these times.

Both men were very witty and each could deliver a punch line without ever cracking a smile!

The young family looked forward to these types of family gatherings and Juanita grew to love Lois Marion's family as much as her own.

Those cane grindings would be treasured memories for all and Uncle E.V.'s coveted cane syrup was a staple for the family table for a lifetime.

Lois Marion was a working mother, keeping her position with the Telephone Company and helping bring in funds for the family. Charles Henry was working for the Power Company as a lineman. Juanita sometimes was left to care for the toddler for short periods of time after her school classes.

At a very young age, Juanita began seeing R.L., a young man from the community and soon into their courtship decided they would marry. Even though her brother and sister-in-law worried she might be too young for marriage, they also felt since their own marriage had begun at 18 and 19 they really couldn't tell Juanita she was too young.

"Practice what you preach!" was the mantra carried by both husband and wife.

R.L. and Juanita were happily married and family photos show the bright and fresh young faces of love. They set up house-keeping in their own little apartment, leaving the young family of three in the little house on Fifth Street alone again and life began anew for both young families.

A New Life – *TheRobertD* arrives...

During the years of R.L.'s military service there came a time when his presence was required overseas and during the times of his absence, the family felt it necessary to move Juanita back into the little house on Fifth Street.

She was now expecting their first child and Charles Henry felt he could better keep her safe if she were back in his home.

Dell Anne was now a five year old and had been somewhat pampered in her short life by aunts, great aunts, great uncles, grandmother (Little Grandmother) and great grandmother (Big Grandmother). Her short life had been filled with family gatherings, church activities, including singing in the children's choir and going to her nursery school.

Lois Marion continued her job with the Telephone Company but was grateful to have her daughter enrolled in a nursery school with Aunt Rhett and Uncle Howard just down the street from the house on Fifth Street.

Dell Anne was always the first child daily to be delivered to Aunt Rhett's and would enjoy sitting in the very tiny kitchen with the older couple who loved all of their very small charges.

Uncle Howard especially loved to seat the child on his lap where she would marvel at his method of drinking his early morning coffee. He would pour a small amount of the black brew from his coffee cup into the saucer underneath and very gently swirl the liquid, blowing gently while he swirled. When cooled enough, he would sip the cooled beverage ever so slowly from his saucer.

The child was mesmerized by this action and although never allowed to taste the brew remarked one day "MY daddy doesn't drink HIS coffee from his 'little plate' like you do!"

Both Aunt Rhett and Uncle Howard laughed heartily at the outburst and happily shared the day's news with the child's young parents upon their arrival.

Apparently Dell Anne was considered somewhat 'precocious' at a young age. She was the only child in the household and knew she was much loved.

During the time of Juanita's pregnancy the couple felt a need to buy a set of bunk beds and allowed Dell Anne to sleep up top while Juanita slept underneath in the lower bunk.

Dell Anne at the time was a sound sleeper and most nights would cause no problems for Juanita in the lower bunk.

One night however apparently the little girl was feeling under the weather; she was quiet and a little feverish if the truth were known. The young parents kissed their little daughter good night and tucked her into her top bunk in the bedroom.

Juanita went to bed in the lower bunk anticipating a good night's sleep.

During the night, the child in the upper bunk began thrashing and making strange sounds, causing Juanita to awaken.

"Dell Anne, honey, are you okay?" she called out to her little niece.

The child did not respond, she merely whimpered so Juanita neared the edge of her lower bunk and called again…"Dell Anne, are you okay?"

As Juanita was gazing upwards in the completely darkened room anticipating the five year old's answer, she heard the little girl move very quickly just as a very strange sound emanated from up above.

YAAAAAAAAAAKKKKKKKKKKK!

In the very next second, as she was gazing upwards towards her niece in the upper bunk, she felt a strange and sticky substance sprayed on her face… something NOT pleasant!

Apparently the little girl had gone to bed with an upset stomach which had soured as the night drew upon them. She was not to the point she could relieve the contents of her little stomach before she went to bed and in fact had slept a bit. However, during her slumber the need to relieve the discomfort had appeared and even though sound asleep, she had somehow leaned over the top railing and filled her aunt's face with the offending remnants of last night's meal!

AARRRGGGGGHHHH!

The child slept so soundly she was only aroused when her mother and father arrived to clean her up!

Juanita was highly offended but learned she should NEVER lean out over her lower bunk peering upwards while her little niece slept above! (Soooooo sorry Nita!)

Dell Anne's status as 'the baby' and all the accoutrements contained within that moniker would soon change however, as Juanita was nearing her due date for her very first child.

There would soon be a NEW baby in their home!

Juanita's term was uneventful although a completely new experience. Her sister-in-law was able to help where necessary to share the burden of the discomfort.

When her due date arrived, Juanita was taken to the local hospital where she delivered a bouncing black haired baby boy on May 5, 1955. Charles

Henry and Lois Marion were ecstatic mother and child were doing so well and prepared yet again for one more addition to their household.

The day the baby boy was brought home from the hospital, the older child, Dell Anne, now knew things were going to be different. She didn't consider this tiny creature an intruder into her world but looked to the baby as being "mine."

She spent hours just sitting and watching him, very interested to watch him being attended to. She was ready to help Juanita or Lois Marion with anything necessary to be done for the new baby.

The little boy was named Robert Dale and would bring much joy into the entire household. He was a very happy child and very rarely cried. When he began to smile at a very early age, Dell Anne took that to mean she could now converse with him and together they would communicate in their own children's ways. She felt she now had her own baby brother and loved spending time with him. Thus began a loving relationship that would remain their entire lives.

Robert Dale had exceptionally large ice blue eyes and with his long coal black hair, was striking as a very young baby. As he grew, it seemed his eyes grew as well and sometimes appeared he would never grow into them. They were huge orbs of blue and much admired, especially since he also had the longest and thickest of eyelashes.

Many ladies would comment they would <u>love</u> to have his eyelashes!

As the baby grew and began rolling over on his own he was placed on a pallet on the floor and the two children kept each other company for long periods of time. The little girl would do something to cause the baby's 'tickle box' to turn upside down and together the pair would sit on the pallet laughing great big children's belly laughs uncontrollably with each other. The adults marveled at how the two got along so well.

The uncontrollable laughter with each other would remain for a lifetime as well.

(However, the strength required to keep it up for very long back then is now waning with the passage of those years! In later years Robert Dale would comment the reason for his uncontrolled mirth was "she looked funny...!"

Oh, TheRobertD, thou remaineth ever the Comedian...)

Hal Henry #2

Soon Juanita and Robert Dale found their own home to await the return of R.L. from his overseas duty tour and the little house on Fifth Street became once more a unit of three. Dell Anne was devastated at the loss of her little brother's presence in their home.

In the spring of 1956 however, Charles Henry and Lois Marion were pleased to learn a new little one was expected. The young couple anxiously awaited the arrival of what they hoped would be the little boy to which they could honor Charles Henry's father, William Henry.

Their first child was to be Hal Henry, however they had lost the opportunity for the name since Dell Anne was a girl. Maybe this time they could use the intended name.

The wait proved difficult since Lois Marion kept her job at the Telephone Company during the early part of her pregnancy but suffered highly with the dreaded morning sickness. She would however, upon the birth of this child, give up her job to become a full time stay at home mother.

She highly anticipated the opportunity.

During her oldest daughter's early years Lois Marion had been an extremely proficient seamstress and loved to create matching mother and daughter dresses and accessories.

In high school she had been quite a proficient seamstress, even winning awards at times for her prowess with the sewing machine. Her sewing was meticulous…slow but extremely exact and to perfection. She relished making their clothing and wearing the matching outfits to church functions and various family outings.

Old black and white photos show a grinning Dell Anne and Lois Marion with matching dresses smiling for the camera. Mother's dress of course was a little more mature without the requisite sash which seemed to be required for little girls' dresses in that era. The young mother had found a pattern for making purses from the old round oatmeal boxes; large for herself and small for her daughter. The material matched their dresses and had pretty little draw strings permitting their treasures to safely rest within.

Dell Anne highly treasured her little purse and preened when the little white hat was placed upon her head.

Dell Anne and Lois Marion in front of Lois Annie's house

The grin on Charles Henry's face, of course, showed his pride in his family when they arrived for Sunday morning services. Many comments were overheard proclaiming Lois Marion's skill with needle and thread.

Their week always began with the Sunday morning church services, lunch with Lois Annie and Clarence, Jr., a second trip back to the church for Sunday evening as well.

They were ardent followers of the Bible and knew they wanted their children to be raised with a strong faith in God. They could always been seen in Prayer Meeting services on Wednesday night as well. Lois Marion sang in the choir and Charles Henry sat in his favorite spot in the auditorium, serving many terms as Deacon and many other positions within the church fellowship as well.

Dell Anne was now in the first grade in school and thoroughly loved her teacher and the opportunity to go to school with all those friends. Those walks to school then back home again with her neighborhood friends were a joy each day. .

During the time of Lois Marion's pregnancy after she had given up her job, a chance came that Dell Anne's teacher had an emergency requiring her to find a substitute teacher in the little community school. Since this treasured teacher was also a friend of the family she thought to ask Lois Marion to help.

It was a very short time for someone to be in the classroom and turned out to be not so much teaching as caretaking the first graders. Lois Marion happily agreed to give it at least her best effort.

She was heavily pregnant and very near her due date, making her condition readily noticeable to the children. Some knew what the large belly meant but some had no clue.

One of Dell Anne's classmates, Betsy, raised her hand in the classroom and asked Lois Marion a very important question. With much sincerity and curiosity she asked Lois Marion. "Teacher...WHY Are you so fat?"

Lois Marion was totally taken aback and was unsure how to proceed with the question. As far as she knew, at these early ages the subject of procreation was not a subject for a first grader.

Gingerly tip-toeing around the subject she gently told the classroom, "Dell Anne is getting a little brother or sister and we are all very happy!" She hoped none of the children would ask any further questions and dared not lock eyes with little Betsy who might take the opportunity to ask for more information.

Fervently she prayed. *Just give me a book...any book...and let me read them a story. Maybe they'll forget about the subject!*

Within reach she found a lovely little book of children's stories and proceeded to turn their attention to something a little more within their age group.

Lois Marion's performance that day took on epic proportions as she read as much drama and interest into that children's story as possible. Her intent was to divert the children's attention to a different subject and she MUST be successful! Otherwise she would be left alone with this room full of children asking questions much too mature and difficult for one very young pregnant lady!

Apparently her performance brought the desired effect on the children and she was able to keep them occupied through the reading until time for playground activities.

With much relief she thought. *Whew; that was one close call! I was scared to death some of those kids might want a show and tell session!*

Upon arriving home that night she shared her day with her husband and they laughingly decided it would be the last substitute teaching position she would ever accept.

After the events of her one and only substitute teaching experience Lois Marion concentrated on preparing for their newest addition to the family, Little Hal Henry #2.

Charles Henry didn't say much when she mentioned if this child would be a boy they would give it the name agreed upon before the birth of their first child.

She kept her options open for whatever they would be given.

April of 1956 brought lovely spring weather and Lois Marion prepared her daughter's Easter frock, always a masterpiece of her sewing talents. She worked tirelessly creating the little dress.

Dell Anne was now six years old and Lois Marion enjoyed her free days while her daughter was in class.

Lois Marion had a first cousin, Lola Jane who had married her high school sweetheart, Grady, and the two couples socialized frequently. They had much in common, even to the point that both men worked at the same power company. This enabled the two men to work and spend social time together as well.

Lois Marion and Lola Jane had been very close as children as well so they too had shared interests which kept both young women busy.

Lola Jane and Grady had been blessed with a son in September of 1948, Donald Grady, who was a favored cousin and playmate of Dell Anne. The two children were just close enough in age to have similar likes and played together famously. Lola Jane and Grady had also been blessed with a second son, Mitchell in 1955.

Since Dell Anne's adopted little brother, Robert Dale, had moved away from the family home, she felt very lonely at times and those occasions when she could play with Donald Grady were treasured and much anticipated.

Donald Grady at a very young age was very active and learned to play those childhood games little boys are so famous for...pushing little cars or blocks of wood through the dirt, imagining he was a cowboy riding a broomstick horse, playing leapfrog over any stump or fence post he could find and climbing any tree in his path.

Dell Anne fell right in beside him and loved all those same types of activities.

Their trips to the country to Great Grandmother Eva's house were greatly anticipated and running barefoot down the soft and sandy ruts of the dirt road was one of the most treasured options. The children would take off very fast in the soft sand and see who could kick up the most sand.

Treasure hunting through the old barns and sheds on Great Grandmother Eva's home-place would bring the children's imaginations to a frenzied flight of fantasy as they played together for hours.

On Grandmother Eva's front porch there lived a treasured sweet potato vine trellised on the west side of the old house and Eva was a master gardener of anything green. Located just in front of that beautiful potato vine was an old porch swing which hung from the rafters and was pleasantly shaded by the abundant leaves of the vines.

The swing would entertain the children as they pushed each other higher and higher on the swing. The squeaking of the chains going back and forth and the squeals of delight from the children would usually bring mothers and fathers to the front door to chastise "Don't you kids swing too high now, if you go through Grandmother Eva's sweet potato vine, she'll skin you alive!"

That quieted the two for a while…most of the time.

Plans had been made that when Lois Marion's delivery time came, Dell Anne would visit with Donald Grady until the baby came and mother and child returned home.

When the day arrived, Charles Henry made sure his daughter was retrieved by Lola Jane and Grady and began the long wait for the newest member of his little family.

Daydreaming periodically he would question himself. *Now will I finally use the name we agreed on for a little boy?* The thoughts of the name Hal Henry was such that his initials would be a very easy "H.H.H" and would be somewhat unique. As he thought of how much he missed his own father he decided it would be very nice to have a son to teach how to farm, fish, play basketball, saw wood and all those things expected of the male in society.

The wait became intolerable and he could only pace the *Father's Waiting Room*. At that time it was not the normal custom for the fathers to be present in the delivery room. That was 'women's work' and therefore men would be considered in the way.

The time arrived on April 16, 1956 when the nurse announced "You have a little…" and he was a smile from ear to ear.

He took the news "GIRL" quite well.

With a great sense of relief Lois Marion's delivery was finally complete as he thought. *Again, no using the name Hal Henry but if she's healthy, it just doesn't matter!*

The young couple had been toying with names all along but secretly settled on the name of Hal Henry if a boy. However the name that was chosen if it was a little girl was 'Charlene' in honor of her father Charles Henry.

No man could be more proud!

Little Charlene was pronounced to be in good health; mother and new baby daughter would stay in the hospital for the requisite three days and would then return home to begin a new life together.

Dell Anne now had her OWN baby!

When the day came for Lola Jane, Grady, Donald Grady and Mitchell to deliver Dell Anne back to her own home, she was thrilled to see her beautiful young mother lounging in a chaise lounge in the cool shade of the covered porch in the little house on Fifth Street.

The little girl raced up the paved sidewalk, up the three steps to the screen door and burst onto the porch hopefully into her mother's waiting arms.

However, the child suddenly noticeably slowed her steps...

With much trepidation and hesitancy to her previously exuberant steps she thought. *Wait...is that Mama? She looks so different...what's wrong and where did that big belly go?* Her mother looked weakened and pale and was no longer wearing the large maternity shirt over her skirts and appeared very thin.

The child slowly moved to her mother's waiting arms and accepted the warm hug her mother was offering but her reticence was a little disconcerting to the adults.

Charles Henry who was by now getting a little concerned at the turn in the child's attitude spoke up, "Well, Mama had the baby and it's a little girl, aren't you happy? You have a little baby sister. She's got blond hair and she's very, very tiny. Do you remember how much fun you had playing with little Robert Dale when he was here? Well, now we have our own baby who will never leave you!"

Dell Anne thought that would be okay so followed her Daddy into the little bedroom to see what was in that little baby bed.

When her Daddy picked her up to present the tiny infant in the little baby bed, she was amazed babies could be so small.

Turning to face her father she asked "Daddy, why doesn't she smile at us like Robert Dale did? Can I play with her now?"

With a smile and kiss upon his daughter's little face he responded "Well no, not now Dell Anne, she's got to grow up a little more before she can smile at you and play with you like a baby doll. You'll just have to have patience but one day you can play together, won't that be nice?"

With total nonchalance to the infant in the baby bed and with her curiosity now completely satisfied she turned her attention to something else...

All adult eyes were on the little girl awaiting her next question or comment but were surprised there would be no further interest in the new addition, at least not at THIS moment.

With much excitement at the prospect, she took her father's hand and led him to the new contraption sitting in the corner of their living room and said "Okay Daddy, now let's go look at the new television you got us!"

And that was that...

Hal Henry #3

After the birth of the second daughter, life continued for the little family on Fifth Street, Dell Anne became a helper to her mother to care for the infant where possible.

Even though initially on the first meeting with the newest member of the family she was more impressed with the new black and white television set in the living room, she became quite adept at fetching baby bottles and clean diapers.

When the infant began smiling as she remembered Robert Dale doing, Dell Anne was more apt to play on the living room pallet with her. She lugged the baby around and kept her occupied while Lois Marion went about her chores as much as possible.

Summers would find Maude's older girls, Barbara and Mary, visiting with their trusty portable phonograph and lots of records in hand. They would arrive on a Greyhound bus with much anticipation of seeing their Uncle's family and days would be filled with music and lots of dancing. The older girls would be allowed to escort Dell Anne to the nearby movie theatre occasionally.

The little girl dearly loved hanging out with them, although their frequent teasing from the cheesy science fiction movies would cause nightmares at times. She was saddened when the girls had to leave but there was always an open invitation for future visits for Charles Henry's nieces and nephews.

Soon Lois Marion began feeling the beginnings of a now familiar nausea coming upon her early in the first year of Charlene's birth and the family realized that yet again they would have a 50/50 chance to use the treasured name of Hal Henry once more.

The day came for Lois Marion's delivery and yet again Charles Henry paced his way in the *Father's Waiting Room* at the local maternity ward.

When the nurse came in and announced the birth of the third child, again Charles Henry wondered if he would be able to use the favored boy's name…

Not to be…Baby Kay Sue was born June 21, 1957, fourteen months after the birth of daughter Charlene. She came into the world a ball of fire, with little to no fine blond hair and quite a temper. Her cries became howls when she wanted attention. While still in infancy she developed a childhood illness with resultant ear infections. The infections would cause fever spikes and convulsions that would place her in the hospital for long periods of time.

These hospitalizations would require Lois Marion to spend countless hours in the infant ward at the local hospital.

Lois Marion and Charles Henry became very concerned at the infant's health but put all their faith into their family doctor and prayed for health and healing. The family went through some difficult times during Kay Sue's first year of life but eventually the medications began to take effect and eventually she left behind the need for the heavy medication previously necessary to save her life.

Her bouts of temper remained and she developed a distinct impatience which sometimes got in her way. At the same time, however she learned very quickly and began doing things toddlers didn't do until much later in their growth patterns.

Lois Marion loved to dress the children in home-made clothes and provided there was time she made as many little outfits as possible. The children grew and the family prospered.

There came a day when Kay Sue was just a toddler and reaching for any and everything. She was extremely curious and was apt to be found under any chair or table within reach.

One day when Charles Henry was holding the youngest infant in his arms, he lit a cigarette and began to take a puff. Before he knew it, Kay Sue had lurched herself up into a very dangerous position in his arms and was on her way to grabbing that hot stick he was holding in his lips.

The quick motion of the baby and his fear she would be burned caused him to quickly reposition her, dropping the burning cigarette from his mouth to the ground.

He had *dodged a bullet* in this instance but vowed he would never again put her or any of his children in harm's way with his smoking habit. He had always been very careful not to smoke while holding his daughters in the past but this time the action just slipped up.

At this time however, he vowed he would stop smoking those cigarettes altogether and told his wife "Marion, throw away those two cartons of Lucky Strikes on the mantel piece; I just can't afford to put these babies in harm's way with my bad habits!"

Lois Marion, with some irritation thought to herself. *Well, Charles, you should have made that decision before I spent the budget on those two cartons...now we've thrown good money after bad!*

She always felt it her duty to budget the grocery money but she always made sure Charles Henry was treated to his vice since he was the one making the household money. She never did abide the habit and told him so when they were dating. He did stop for a while when they were dating but over the years had picked up the habit once again.

This time however, the decision had been made by his little daughter. If he didn't have that stick in his mouth to pique her curiosity then he wouldn't be damaging his child with his bad habit.

That decision to stop smoking *cold turkey* would remain the rest of his days and we have Kay Sue to thank for that...

Bustin' out the Windows

After the birth of the third child, Kay Sue, the couple found their treasured little house on Fifth Street just could not contain all those daughters so Charles Henry decided he would try his hand at construction.

He planned to add a master bedroom and a special all-purpose room. The two rooms would be built onto the north end of the home, replacing existing windows with doors and would feature lovely tongue in groove pine paneling, hardwood floors, a built in book shelf for his treasured books and a large closet for Lois Marion's frocks.

He vowed to do his best and studied all manner of construction drawings then set about building the new addition with all the exuberance youth has to offer.

He had no father to help lead him through the new experience but his devotion to his young wife and his three daughters was pushing him to accomplish this new experience. He did, however, totally trust the opinion and recommendations of his mother in law Lois Annie since she had been a very valued employee of the local lumber yard over the years and knew many construction workers.

She had even had her own treasured little home built after she lost her husband in World War II. He would trust her judgment and she could point out the best prices available for the materials.

Charles Henry was employed as a lineman with the Power Company and worked very hard, manual work on his day job which ended at 4:30 each afternoon. He would rush home to his prepared evening meal then would be found sawing, nailing and working hard and heavy well into the evenings.

In the beginning the only light came from a floor lamp (minus the shade) which lit the way until such time each night as he felt he could no longer bother the neighbors with the noise.

The days ended with a quick bath, a kiss for each of his girls then straight to bed to rest for yet another round the next day.

The work was difficult, tedious and at times left him wondering what in the world was he thinking when he began the project. Of course, his devotion to his girls would drive him ever further to its completion.

Months of this daily routine took its toll on the family; Lois Marion trying her best to keep the toddlers out of harm's way from nails and construction debris and Dell Anne longing for the day when she could slide across the slippery floors in stocking feet.

The day finally arrived when all the paneling was up, lights were installed, windows were operational and the beautiful oak floors were down, varnished and polished into a beautiful high gloss.

Donald Grady arrived on this Saturday and Charles Henry and Lois Marion allowed the two children to run and slide across the empty room on those beautiful slippery floors. Of course, they could only play for a few hours in this manner since Grady and Lola Jane had arrived to help move the furniture into the proper rooms. The adults, however, did allow the two youngsters their moments of frivolous fun.

Many bumps and bruises were endured by both children that only hurt after their play concluded.

Charles Henry had found a lovely unfinished wood 9 drawer dresser which he lovingly varnished to a high gloss.

He had utilized the opening of two windows for doorways, one near the fireplace of the home and the other into the back bedrooms and bathroom of the home. This pathway would eventually make for wondrous runways for all the children as they chased one another around and around the house.

Of course, by this time, regardless of the fact Lois Marion was now a young mother of three little girls it did NOT stop her from chasing her oldest daughter around and around the house as well!

Dell Anne was privileged to have been the first born of her mother and father at their ripe old ages of twenty and nineteen respectively. Lois Marion was still young and active enough to run and play just like her eight year old daughter and took every occasion to do so.

The construction of the addition to the home was a success and Lois Marion was highly proud of her husband's building skills and accomplishments! He sacrificed much for his young love and she stood behind him proudly watching him mature into a devoted husband and family man.

She was proud to recall all those people who had said at their young marriage "It will never last, they are just too young!" In her heart she knew this marriage would last their entire lifetimes!

There were dancing lessons for Dell Anne at the local Women's Club down on Lake Isabella, many hours of fun in the summers at the nearby swimming pool, lots of fun with buddies Renny and Becky on bicycles, roller skates and just running and climbing.

Much time was spent playing but much time was also allocated to helping her mother with the babies.

Sunday church services were always treasured by the family since it would bring Lois Annie back to their home for Sunday dinner and an afternoon of rest. The church singing was highly enjoyed by all, including the little girl, Dell Anne who took to music very early in life.

Family outings were enjoyed tremendously by the children when they would go to the frequent dinners on the grounds for reunions, church lunches and those 'just because' times of fellowship.

They were born into an extremely large extended family and the reunions were frequent. Lois Annie came from a family of 15 children total who now had children and grandchildren of their own as well.

Lola Jane and Grady had increased their brood by one more birth with Sharon who was the age of Kay Sue. Each child had a buddy in those years and all loved to play together whenever possible.

The local movie theatre (the same one in which their parents had courted in their youth) was a very strong draw for Dell Anne and Donald Grady. They were old enough and the proximity of the theatre was close enough in this very small and safe community to walk all by themselves down to the theatre. They paid their quarters for admittance to the cowboy matinee and still had enough left over to buy a *Coke* and a bag of popcorn.

They would try to be the first ones into the theatre on those days and would rush down the aisle to the one of only two double seats in that old auditorium. There they would sit sharing their popcorn and *Coke* and enjoy the wonderful old movies of Roy Rogers, Dale Evans, Gene Autry, Gabby Lynn Hayes and of course her very favorite, Hop-Along Cassidy.

Life was simple and sweet in those days although to the young couple working to make a living, keeping a safe roof over their heads and food on the table for their 'cubs', there were struggles then and more would later arrive as well.

They would still demand however…NO credit.

Trips down south to visit with Maude and Juanita would bring shrieks of joy when the children learned there was to be a road trip. Maude had increased her family with the birth of another son, Richard and Nita had increased her family with the birth of Lisa Gail.

Maude lived in Tampa and Nita lived in St. Petersburg which allowed Charles Henry and his band of 'cubs' to visit both while in the area.

Those trips were exciting, at times difficult since the prevalent conversation of the youngsters in the car as soon as the car was put into drive was "Daddy, are we there yet?" Better yet, the frequent "Daddy, we have to go to the litter box" was also quite common.

(For years the comment upon passing the frequent I-75 rest areas would find Charles Henry hollering to his girls "Anybody need to scratch? Speak now or hold it till the next rest stop!")

Sometimes on the way back up north, the car would contain a member of either Maude's family or Nita's family for a little visit. He was intent on keeping a tight bond with his sisters and their families and shared frequently.

During the spring of 1958 Lois Marion began feeling those old familiar feelings of nausea once more.

Oh, my word, will THIS one finally be a little Hal Henry?

Hal Henry #4

The summer months were extremely difficult for the young mother and even though her daughter was a help to her, some things just could not be done by anyone but the mother.

The months of nausea had taken their toll on her body and she felt at times completely overcome by the demands of a household, a husband, three children and another on the way.

She fervently hoped this birth would be without incident and the baby, whatever the gender, would be safe and healthy.

The bi-weekly paycheck was beginning to show signs of stress in budgeting for the children, the resultant expenses of Kay Sue's medical condition and the construction of the new rooms. All had put a sizable dent into their little nest egg.

At the birth of the second daughter, Charles Henry had fenced the entire yard of the little house on Fifth Street to help his young wife keep the children safe and contained within the confines of their own property.

The necessity of the daily washing of diapers and baby clothing took a toll on Lois Marion since there always seemed to be something to wash, iron, fold, repair or put away at any given moment. She did her best to keep up with the mountains of housework and Dell Anne was instructed to keep an eye on her baby sisters at every turn possible.

She still, however, wanted her older child to be able to play with her friends as much as she could as well.

As it was, at this time in life, Dell Anne was most days expected to arrive home from school with her dress gathers pulled completely out from under her sash. She loved to play leapfrog on the school playground. Those days of leapfrog would place her hands in just the right spot to rip the entire fronts out of her dresses each time she found a tree stump to jump over which meant to Lois Marion yet one more repair job!

Lola Jane and Lois Marion had put their heads together in hopes of trying to come up with some kind of stay at home business to make a little extra money. Lola Jane began making cakes and Lois Marion set her mind to learning how to decorate birthday and wedding cakes.

She studied all manner of cakes and looked for just the right recipe to make the decorating icing. This creative project would one day be her at-home work and would help to supplement the family checkbook.

In later years she would become an extremely proficient baker and cake decorator and for years would be called upon to make all manner of cakes, including many of the wedding cakes for the events in their town. There was no in-grocery bakery and the one and only bakery in town produced only donuts and cookies.

As the time drew near for her last delivery and with the heaviness of her pregnancy she began to experience much leg pain and could not stand for very long at a time. Her legs would swell as she began developing varicose veins in her lower legs.

These symptoms were troublesome but she found if she could just sit down for a little and rest she would eventually be able to once again stand and do her various chores.

The day came in late January of 1959 that the opportunity to once again use the name of Hal Henry was near.

The young couple decided this would have to be the last, regardless of the gender. They had not especially planned any of their children; God just sent them when he saw fit.

The day Lois Marion was to be delivered came on January 27, 1959 and once again, there would be no use for the name of Hal Henry.

Little Nola Jane was born and the couple decided to put away any intentions of ever expecting to use a little boy's name,

She was a tiny baby girl with a head full of black, black curls, much like the first little girl and was a very calm child who would grow to be especially close to her older sister, Kay Sue. They would only be nineteen months apart which fact would confuse people at times since they looked very much alike as they grew. Many people would mistake them for twins during their youth.

"Well, are you going to try again for a little boy?" A very kind and caring visitor to her hospital bedside asked the young mother of now four little girls.

Lois Marion without hesitation and in a very clear and adamant voice replied "Well, all I can say is I WILL NOT fill up my back yard with little girls just to get ONE little boy!"

And that was that...

The Early Years

As the little family grew, the three youngest daughters who were so close in ages grew as 'stairsteps' in height. The oldest child referred to the three younger as 'the doorsteps' since the only thing she could relate to the moniker given by various acquaintances was the entrances to their little home which had three steps. Besides, her parents always referred to the front 'doorsteps' or the back 'doorsteps' as well.

The name stuck when referring to the three as a group.

Acquaintances would comment how cute they all were with their home-made matching outfits.

The three youngest children used that treasured 'running path' through the little home their father had recently constructed and when they had enough of running inside, they retired to the yard where Lois Annie had purchased a merry-go-round, sand box and climber. The three played for hours out in the front yard on those beloved play-sets.

Charles Henry had purchased some of the old power poles being replaced on the roadways and built a huge swing in the side yard as well and many hours were spent swinging to the heavens.

During late 1959 after the birth of the youngest daughter, Lois Marion began in earnest to build her cake decorating business and developed quite a healthy customer base.

Dell Anne was designated to be the 'cleaner-upper' of the icing bags which required standing at the kitchen sink and melting out MANY icing bags with hot water. The neighborhood children would arrive at the back doorsteps when alerted to the possibility of treats and appeared as baby birds with open mouths to await the possibility of just a little squirt of the luscious icing. Dell Anne was always willing to share the sweet concoctions and Lois Marion had asked the neighborhood mothers if they minded their children receiving the icing.

No one seemed to mind so Dell Anne shared.

One day there had been a fairly large cake order which required many varied colors of icing. Dell Anne decided to mix all the colors together and see just what color might appear.

Well… it appeared as DIRT.

When the time arrived for the neighborhood 'chicks' to appear for their treats, they took one look at the color and ALL refused to partake.

They were absolutely certain Dell Anne had removed any icing from those bags and replaced it with plain and simple DIRT…

No manner of cajoling or promising it was in fact their favored icing would convince any one of them to even take a taste to prove it was real! That day proved more cumbersome for Dell Anne's clean up chore since she had to discard a huge amount of the treasured icing before she could begin the melting and cleaning of those nasty bags.

The tasting parties continued, however mother and daughter decided no more mixing colors ever again!

Lois Marion's business was picking up, actually earning extra income and Charles Henry decided in order to give his family what he had NOT had, it would be necessary to do something to increase his checkbook.

He was proud of his little home and his family but knew he wanted to give them more. His father, William Henry had passed this life never having owned a home of his own and was helpless to offer financial support to his own children.

However, Charles Henry heeded his father's word. "Son, do everything you can to make sure you give your children a safe roof over their heads and make sure that home is YOURS, paid in full as early as you can!" he preached.

Charles Henry was an avid student and knew what he had to do to move forward in his path to success. He needed to buy a farm. He determined he would turn back to the earth for those bounties he knew he could provide.

Lois Marion had been raised on a farm and had vowed she did NOT want to be a farmer's wife; she knew the hardships endured.

In their dating years Charles Henry had asked her at one time "Would you marry a farmer?"

Her reply was a simple "Depends on who the farmer is!"

However, Charles Henry had no intention of giving up his position with the power company; he would add to his family income by growing crops. If he played his cards right he just might be able to one day have enough money to completely pay off his homestead and all debts. His goal was to have this accomplished by the age of fifty.

He began an upward-mobile course of action that would greatly increase his fortune and enhance the lives of his family.

Very early Lois Marion found she could not dissuade her husband from his plans to move to the farm so instead focused on the promised new home he was to build her. It would be large, very lovely and would prove his devotion to her and their children.

He found the first farm on Highway 47, south of the little community and bought a beautiful 80 acre farm complete with a heavy stand of mature pecan trees.

He began to till the land and heard of a State plan to purchase land to build a super highway through the State of Florida. To his great pleasure he found the State wanted to purchase a corner of his new property to accomplish the new Interstate 75 project.

This was extremely joyous news since it gave him enough funds to begin construction of the beautiful new red brick home within the stand of those stately old pecan trees. It would feature four bedrooms and a bathroom for just the children. There would be a master bathroom just for him...*finally, a bathroom I don't have to share with four little girls!*

They both felt so blessed to have a beautiful home with both a huge living and family room as well. She was also to be blessed with a brand new dishwasher; something she could only dream of!

Coming from the little house on Fifth Street, the overall size of the home was twice larger and the young family was able to move into their new abode in 1961.

All sights were set on their future and Charles Henry began to plan just what crops with which he would begin his new endeavor.

He was very proud of his choice, summer squash, and knew the day would come very soon to harvest. He was a little worried about the market at the time however since it appeared many other farmers had the same idea that year. Silently he feared the market would be flooded if everyone harvested at the same time. He knew farming was somewhat of a gamble but it was a price he had to pay in order to move up the ladder of success.

He also knew whatever choice he made there would be a 50/50 chance to make a profit.

When the time came for harvest he filled up his little Chevrolet pickup truck with beautiful yellow squash and Lois Marion volunteered her services to deliver his crops to market. He had already been in contact with a market in a northeastern metropolis sixty miles away from them. He had a buyer and the only thing left to do was to drive them over and deliver the goods.

Lois Marion set out with her youngest child in the front seat of a fully loaded pickup truck of beautiful yellow crookneck squash. She would drive the miles, deliver her young husband's crop, return in time to greet her three daughters home from their classes then together they would figure their first profits from his farming venture.

The day began like any other, her excitement at being able to do this job for her husband was strong and she knew she would be there to help out when he needed her. He had to go to his day job with the Power Company so she would be responsible for delivery.

She could surely do that!

Upon her arrival at the market where the promised sale was to be delivered she found to her horror that the store manager would NOT take delivery as promised. Apparently as Charles Henry had feared, the market WAS flooded. His crop had arrived too late. A day in the life of a farmer can be devastating if he can't get his goods to market first.

She was horrified!

With a sickness deep in the pit of her stomach she worried. *How in the world can I drive back home with all these vegetables in the truck; where can I go, what can I do with them?* She had learned to trust his business instinct and knew since she was already far from home; she HAD to do something with all those goods. She would NOT let her husband down in her self-appointed task.

She determined she and her child would drive in the truck in that huge, unfamiliar town, stop at each and every market she could find and try to sell them on her own! He had worked far too hard and long for her to walk away from an inconvenience now.

The day was long, her child was weary and <u>she</u> was weary as she went to every single market she could find once more asking the question "Sir, can YOU buy my squash today?" This took a lot of courage on the part of one very shy and quiet young mother, especially in a time this type of marketing was usually done by males.

By late afternoon and dealing with a grumpy little one in the truck she realized she was not having any luck at all and had to cease her attempts at selling the goods. Besides, her other daughters would be arriving home to an empty house and that did not set well with her.

She had always made it her business to be home to welcome each and every one of them to assure their safe arrivals home. She turned the truck back to the west and cried softly the entire way home.

Once Charles Henry arrived home and heard of the horrible day his young wife had and of the seriously bad news of the crops he took her in his arms where she sobbed uncontrollably.

He gently comforted her and with sadness he said "Well, honey, that's okay, I guess I just didn't pick the right crop this year…we'll get through this and we'll be okay. I knew there would be a chance we wouldn't make it on the first try but that's the way farming goes; one year you might make a good profit, the next year you might do good to come out even and one year you just might lose everything. That's okay, it's not going to stop us; we will forge ahead and try something else next year" he promised.

With tears in her eyes she looked up into her husband's beautiful green eyes and asked "But what will we do with all those squash in the truck…do we have to just throw them away? We can't possible eat <u>all</u> of them, can we?"

"Well no, Bride, we'll eat as many as we can, share with our family and neighbors and what we can't give away will have to go to the wild critters in the fields. I'm sure <u>something</u> will enjoy them!"

That year brought many squash casseroles, buttered squash, fried squash, squash fritters, squash bread, baked squash with cream of chicken soup and any other recipes she could find; (too, too, WAY TOO MANY!)

The spring of the next year brought an experience with nature that can only be described as sheer terror.

The young farmer had begun constructing a huge back porch on the rear of their brick home with intentions of placing a roof and screens around the perimeter of the room. He had already laid a ledge of brick about two feet high upon which the structure and support system for the roof was to be installed.

The construction was done on his off time and he knew it would take a few months to complete the structure but meant it to be a place by mid-summer where he could rest in the cool of the afternoon. It was a very long and wide structure and would provide much shade for the home.

Periodically Charles Henry hired a young girl on Saturdays to help Lois Marion with her various duties around the house and on this day the washing caused many trips to be made to the clothesline. Upon each trip to the clothesline, the young girl noticed the dog, Goldie, barking at something near the ledge of the new porch but did not go over to check it out until a few trips into the day.

The barking of the dog, however, became increasingly more urgent and she finally traversed closer to where the problem seemed to lie.

The three youngest daughters were sitting on the concrete slab playing jacks and were totally oblivious to the dog's incessant barking. They were all of the ages of 3, 4 and 5 and the danger was poised less than four feet from their location on the other side of the ledge.

To the horror of the young hired helper, she ran to Lois Marion who was washing dishes in the kitchen and told her "The dog has found a snake in the yard and I think you'd better come <u>right now!</u>"

The young farmer was next door at the neighbor's property at least a quarter mile down the road but close enough to hear shouts from one property to the other.

Lois Marion took a peek toward the dog which by this time was becoming more and more aggressive towards something in the grass. The family lawn mower had been broken for some weeks and the grass unfortunately had become quite high at that point.

When Lois Marion realized this was not just a snake but a <u>rattlesnake,</u> the adrenaline kicked in and she was bent on protecting her children.

She hoped Goldie would be able to keep the snake's attention long enough to quietly get the little girls' attentions and have them move very slowly away from the ledge.

The now coiled HUGE rattlesnake was attempting to strike the raging dog who was fighting fiercely for her family.

Lois Marion prayed she could get the children to move slowly without giving away the secret that danger was near. She feared if any one of them went into a 'meltdown' she couldn't protect them without leaving one in harm's way. They grudgingly complied and moved from that location, never having an inkling the snake was in the vicinity.

The young wife then told Dell Anne who was now twelve "Run to the pack house and get a hoe...I have to kill that snake!"

The older daughter ran as fast as she could to get the necessary implement to help. Unfortunately the supply of farming equipment at the moment was somewhat limited and there was only one hoe to be found. She grabbed it and ran as fast as she could to her mother.

Lois Marion stealthily climbed atop the ledge and inched her way toward the coiled snake. To her horror, she realized the thing was HUGE, even fully coiled. *This is no baby snake* she realized with horror...*this is a Grandpa snake and I HAVE to get him away from my babies...NOW!*

Goldie was doing a GREAT job at keeping the snake occupied so the young housewife inched closer and closer and with all the might she possessed brought the sharp edge of the hoe down upon the snake's head...

WHAP went the hoe and the force of the impact on such a huge snake merely *bounced up*, sending the young mother into overdrive!

With adrenalin pumping she began in earnest to remove the life from that dreaded snake and with each strike, screamed at the top of her lungs **"CCCHHHAAARRLLLEEESSSS..."**

Dell Anne and the three younger girls could only stare in fear and wonder that their mother had found so much strength to chop that snake up!

WHAP... **"CCCHHHAAARRLLLEEESSSS..."** **WHAP...**"CHH AARLLEESS..."*WHAP...* **"CCCHHHAAARRLLLEEESSSS..."** could be heard across the farm in a high pitched, hysterical tone and to his horror and fear the farmer realized *THAT SOUND IS COMING FROM MY FARM!*

He ran across the pasture located between the neighboring home and each *WHAP* of the hoe across the snake's head brought another ear splitting **"CHARLES..."** yet again!

By the time he arrived to the rear of their home, he saw his beautiful young wife standing tall on the ledge with an old hoe in her hand chopping the daylights out of something in the grass!

She was still *WHAPPING* and SCREAMING, never even noticing he had now arrived! Her face was completely white and her hair was wet around the edges. She was covered in sweat from the exertion of handling that weapon of mass destruction!

She was in absolute terror!

When she noticed her husband had now arrived, she relinquished the hoe to him and he went about completing the job she had started on the dangerous snake!

Her legs went out from under her and she was trembling uncontrollably! She found a seat on the steps leading into the house and cried uncontrollably while her husband tended to the remainder of the snake. She held her three babies close in relief and vowed to make sure Goldie received a reward for notifying them of the danger.

When she spoke to her husband and told him she wasn't sure if she had killed the snake or not he loudly guffawed and said "Well, Mama, you didn't just kill him...<u>YOU WORRIED HIM TO DEATH!</u>"

He was mighty proud that little woman had done so much to protect their children and vowed to make sure a sharper hoe would be within range if there was a next time! He now could be assured she would do whatever necessary to protect their daughters.

He held her close, soothing her fear and thanking God for all of their safety. The instance could have been a horrible death if any of the children had been struck by that huge snake. The size of the snake proved indeed it was a fully matured and OLD snake which could have caused much heartache within his family!

Again, this little quiet, shy and retiring girl would shock his being to the core when he learned yet another trait in his wife. *She not only has a set of lungs on her...she has muscles of steel as well!*

Charles Henry began to search for some other type of crops or livestock with which to forge his future. He concentrated on what might be his next venture. *Maybe a...'I know...I'll buy a milking cow! We can make our own butter and sell the milk we don't use. That will help our budget a little bit at least!"*

With that tidbit of information Lois Marion cringed…thinking to herself. *Now I'm REALLY in for some trouble!*

(Left to right) Dell Anne, Lois Marion on back row,
Charlene, Charles holding Kay Sue and Nola Jane

When the time came for him to purchase a milk cow, he chose a beautiful tan and white colored cow already heavily pregnant with calf. The family of little girls of course had to give her a name so someone came up with the name of 'Tiny.' (She WASN'T!)

When the calf was born and the time arrived to begin milking her, Charles Henry milked the old cow before work and upon his arrival home each evening.

However, due to an extremely bad work accident in 1964 and his subsequent recuperation causing a one year absence from his job, the need arose for Lois Marion to take over the farm work and milk Tiny twice each day.

Lois Marion had milked cows in the past and it wasn't difficult. However, Tiny had a mind of her own and would misbehave, usually just when the pail was almost full of that luscious creamy milk. The family had all the fresh milk they could use or sell, fresh buttermilk was abundant and she and the children would even make their own butter from the cream of the fresh milk.

Hours were spent by the children simply sitting and shaking mayonnaise jars full of the rich cream until it was just right and the beautiful butter would be ready for salting. At one point the family invested in a simple paddle-installed butter churn and many afternoons found the children turning the handle of the big old red-lidded churn, eager to help.

The routine for this young housewife was to get her children up, cook their breakfasts which ALWAYS included grits, eggs, fresh ham or bacon, homemade biscuits and again, the treasured cane syrup, then see to her injured husband. She would assure the three older girls were dressed and had all the daily accoutrements for their school day, then were ready and waiting for the school bus in front of their house.

Only after all this work would she become ready to milk that dreaded cow!

Her breakfast dishes would wait and any housework, clothes washing (she had to hang all their clothes on the clothes line), clothing repair or cake decorating orders would have to be rearranged to suit the needs of Tiny…

The cold mornings were the absolute worst; she would put on her oldest but warmest outer clothing, farm boots and gloves in hopes today's milking would not be an episode to remember. Lois Marion had always been a very meek and mild lady but was not above doing hard labor either. She knew she would have to do whatever was needed and she was up for the challenge.

Her devotion to her green eyed husband was very challenging at times but she loved him with all her heart and would do anything to help him succeed in his endeavors.

One morning in the very coldest of the year, (actually sleeting at the time) she trudged out to the barn and began the hated milking.

She tied the cow to the milking post and began her morning chore.

Tiny was apparently feeling the cold as well and began to dance around while Lois Marion was milking. The old cow attempted to throw her head back and 'horn' her at various times sending the young woman into a tizzy. She normally did not show much anger but that too was building in her on this cold and sleeting morning.

With much grit she swore to herself. *Just you wait old Tiny…I'LL get the better of you today!*

When the bucket was almost full and she was beginning to see the light at the end of the tunnel and dreaming of the warmth of her home, she noticed the old cow trying to turn her horns back toward her yet again. When milking a cow, a farmer knows to remain as far away from those horns as possible and she had been vigilant. She moved to one side to escape a jab of the cow's horns just at the time the cow put her nasty foot right in the middle of the milk pail!

All that lovely milk now was totally spoiled and would need to be discarded; she couldn't possibly use it for anything after the cow's foot had been in it! With total aggravation she thought. *No milk, no butter, no nothing; all on the coldest dang day of the year! What a waste!*

Her ire got the better of her and with both hands she grabbed old Tiny's head and twisted just as hard as she could!

The old cow seemed dazed and truth be known the surprise of Lois Marion's attack must have come as a total shock. If the old cow had been alert, the young woman's efforts at wringing her neck would have met with a huge resistance. As it was, the surprise showed who the real victor was on this cold day and very quickly settled Tiny right down!

(Not sure but old Tiny might have seen stars that day!)

Lois Marion determined she would NOT let the cow win THIS one!

When told of the morning's events, Charles Henry with a loud guffaw told her "WELL, I GUESS YOU SHOWED OLD TINY WHO'S BOSS, DIDN'T YOU, LOVE?"

For hours afterwards, every time he looked at his wife's beautiful form, his face broke into a huge grin and she could hear his chuckle over and over again!

She, however, did NOT find the instance as comical as he!

Life Goes On

As the girls grew and life progressed on the new farm, Charles Henry grew many different crops over the years, the most profitable being that of farming tobacco. The entire family got into the raising of this particular crop, summers requiring extremely early morning rising. They had to remove the cooked tobacco from the barn in preparation for the day's green tobacco to replace within.

Lola Jane and Grady added another daughter, Anita to their family and Juanita added Sandy to her family. Maude had completed her family by 1950.

Charles Henry's three nephews, Junior and Richard, Maude's two sons and Robert Dale from his sister Juanita returned to the farm to help work the crops and make extra money from their school holidays.

Junior was the oldest of the children and functioned as the foreman of the workers, taking charge while Charles Henry worked his job with the Power Company.

During the cold winter months there was only the family of husband, wife and four little girls to plant, protect with plastic from the harsh freezing cold then replant into the fields when the young plants were hardy enough.

When school classes let out in the summer however, the three young boys traveled to their Uncle's farm to work all summer long. The family welcomed those boys not just for the work they did but for the fun they brought as well.

Those days were hard, hot and miserable work days at times but the family of girls loved having the boys come to live with them in the summers. Frolicking in the nearby springs after a hard day's work was much anticipated as well as all the fun times brought by the family comedian Robert Dale.

Robert Dale was always tall and thin and wore thick black glasses most of his childhood and with his beautiful huge ice blue eyes had learned how to use those eyes to his advantage very well. He was very vocal and loved to tease. Most of the time what came out of his mouth was absolutely unexpected but extremely comedic even at his young age.

He loved to try to *get to* his Uncle with his surprising wit and most times would receive a very stern look but no reaction. However, when Robert was out of 'earshot' Charles Henry would loudly guffaw and marvel at his nephew's comedy!

Robert also had a very special talent the girls loved to witness.

He was extremely limber and was able to sit on the floor, lock both legs around the back of his <u>own neck</u> and lift himself with his long and thin arms completely off the floor! He would walk on his hands in this method, swinging his butt as he moved and the entire family would be rolling in the floor in laughter!

(The images of these instances are bringing tears of laughter at this writing and upon the occasion many years later when asked if he could still accomplish this feat he replied simply but adamantly "Not even trying sister!)

Of course, times sitting on the old tractor during breaks in the work day brought much singing by Junior of "Duke, Duke, Duke, Duke of Earl, Duke, Duke, Duke of Earl" for those who may remember the old 1962 song.

Richard and Junior were great wrestlers and spent many hours practicing moves on each other and shouts of "Do you give...? Do you give...?" were heard on regular occasions. Charles Henry loved to see his nephews rolling around on the floor and his green eyes sparkled with mirth to watch them.

"HARRR, HARRRR, HARRR" he would roar. "Mama, look at them boys, that Richard knows a good way to get to Junior, don't he? Each one gives as good as he gets!"

There were frolicking days of swimming in the Itchetucknee Springs after chores were completed just like Charles Henry and his buddies had done so long ago.

The family worked from before sun-up to very late in the afternoon. When Charles Henry returned home from his job he would jump in to help finish up all the work for the day just as if he had all the energy in the world. The oldest children cropped tobacco, handed and strung up the green leaves then stayed to place all those sticks back into the fresh barn for another week's cooking. Robert Dale was privileged to be taught how to drive that huge old tractor pulling the required tobacco sled. He would literally have to STAND on the brakes when needing to stop the monster. He may have been thin and wiry but he was DETERMINED to do a good job for his Uncle Charles.

Charles Henry would assure all his cooking barns were running at optimum capacity and prayed for a profitable year. His wife cooked the many meals and continued her cake baking business as well as the mountains of housework.

In the meantime he had added to his farming and income producing plans by raising hogs, chickens, turkeys, quail, guinea hens and cows, not to mention enough vegetables to furnish food for the entire county for the season. He was very generous with his vegetables and offered the bounty of his fields to any and all. If he heard of someone who could use a good meal, he harvested, cleaned, cooked then delivered the bounty as his neighborly duty.

He had vowed to his young love all those years ago "<u>My</u> children will NEVER go hungry!"

He was a man of his word and worked hard to include his friends and acquaintances as well. He remembered all those nights of going to bed hungry in his own youth and vowed he would do all he could to share with others.

The fall and early winter would bring harvests of the huge stand of mature pecan trees. The couple allowed the children to keep the profits of their dreaded toil in picking up pecans. This task provided their spending money for Christmas presents to each other.

All worked hard for what they received but were always pleased and proud to receive any and all.

Many late fall Saturday mornings would find Charles Henry with a very long cane fishing pole knocking the mature nuts from the branches. The harvest would come crashing down into the cool grass beneath allowing even the youngest to pick up her share of the nut meats.

Lois Marion had begun suffering early in life with varicose veins in her legs but even this back breaking task would find her in the yard as well. No one would be left out of any chores necessary to help the family succeed toward their goals.

Even with all the work, hardship, pain and suffering of injuries, bad luck with crops, weather damage or the necessary day to day requirements of having a home, farm and family, nothing would stop the trips to their home church every Sunday and Wednesday.

They attended the same church in which years earlier they had repeated their lifelong vows to each other… "Until death do us part."

The couple required their daughters to be active in the church, tithe, and love each other. Sunday still brought Lois Annie to their home in the country for Sunday dinner. Before they left at 8:30 AM on Sunday mornings to attend church services, Charles Henry could be found in the kitchen preparing his specialty oven roast with carrots, potatoes and celery. This banquet would be placed into the oven and cooked over slow heat while the family worshipped.

He had become an excellent cook of anything he put his hand to and many acquaintances were pleased to partake of his bountiful table. No one would be allowed to open the lid of that roasting pan too early. If the heat and steam were to escape, the meat would not be allowed to 'rest' in its own juices and would ruin the quality of the roast. If left to 'rest a spell' it would be so tender one could cut it with a fork.

By the family's arrival home after services, the only thing left to do to prepare the noon day meal (dinner) would be to heat up the vegetables prepared before-hand, cut fresh tomatoes and cucumbers in the summer and of course, Lois Marion had to make her by now famous home-made biscuits for lunch. (The highly desired cane syrup was always close by as well.)

There were many times however, when it would be Lois Marion's turn to prepare the Sunday meal. Those days she might be found frying her wonderful southern fried chicken cut the old fashioned way with the wishbone and breast separated.

On those days there would be 'dibs called' by the children on the favored pieces of chicken. One daughter called dibs on "the thigh, the heart and the gizzard" and the others would 'call dibs' on the favored "white bone" or the piece with the breast cartilage.

Mother and Grandmother would take whatever was left and Charles Henry would ALWAYS call the neck and the backbone.

(Everyone thought back then they were his <u>favored</u> pieces of the chicken when in reality and only learned when the girls grew up and had their own children, he actually desired <u>his family</u> to take the best pieces first! Even back then he was devoted to all his girls but he must have really been pleased to pick the <u>best</u> pieces of chicken after they left the nest!)

In the winter they enjoyed the wonderful turnip, collard or mustard greens from the garden and the requisite home-made corn bread with which they sopped up the 'pot liquor.'

Those days were hard but the couple always shared the bounty of their labors with their friends, family and anyone invited to share.

There were many Sunday mornings of impromptu invitations to other families, "Why don't ya'll follow us home for dinner? We have plenty; you know you're always welcome!" The family was very social and invited others to partake of meals with them at every given opportunity.

The general saying when arriving at their table was "If you leave Charlie's table hungry…it's your own fault!"

The meal time prayer was always offered by Charles Henry and would begin "Lord, pardon our sins and make us thankful for these and all our many blessings."

Upon the attendance of family or friends and immediately after he had completed Grace he would look at each and every member of that table and say "We are just as <u>proud</u> to have all of you here with us!"

A favored Uncle many times would be present at the table and the children delighted in saying right after prayer "Dig in, Uncle Pat!" And ALWAYS after that remark "I WANT A HORSE" from baby Nola Jane.

It was also during these times that Lois Marion's cake decorating business was taking off and she many days had a cake of some kind cooling on the table.

Charles Henry used to grouse in jest to anyone who would listen "I am the only man in the world who has to eat his meals with fourteen cakes around his elbows but NEVER gets a bite!" As the girls grew they used to tease their daddy that he would smell the aromas from the kitchen when she was baking her precious sour cream pound cakes, and would purposely slam the back door on his way in!

He always denied this practice but also was very aware when one of those luscious cakes 'fell' then he would get the one she couldn't deliver! (Everyone should experience the taste of a 'fallen' sour cream pound cake at least once in their lives, especially the ones with coconut flavoring!)

The jokes and laughter abound in the home, the family had their little spats and normal aggravations but the girls grew into respectful adults.

Charles Henry and Lois Marion were proud of their girls and even though they never had an occasion to name any one of their 'cubs' Hal Henry, they were proud to see their girls grow and mature.

When asked years later if he had been sorry he never had a boy to carry on his name he said "Honestly, you know I wouldn't change a one of my girls...I'm just happy to have all four of them well, safe and happy! No, I never regretted any one of them!"

(Besides the fact he didn't have to have boys to make farmers at all; those girls could tote irrigation pipes just as good as any boys!) Farm life was good to them and when the oldest graduated from high school and left for her first job in a city far to the southeast of their community, they concentrated on helping the younger three succeed in their school work.

The oldest had been far too headstrong or as Charles Henry called her "firm headed" and did not want to pursue a college education. She felt if her daddy had been able to succeed by the sweat of his brow, then she too could do the same!

This fact was a sorrow for the couple however since they wanted to offer more than they had received in their youth and could only stand aside and hope she would make the right decisions for her future.

For the younger three, however, they vowed to push the education subject a little harder on them. They were much more social in their junior and high school years and were well liked by their peers, gaining high marks in their studies their entire school years.

The future was bright for all.

Time for a Change

After the oldest daughter left the family nest Charles Henry decided he needed to purchase a larger tract of land. He was a visionary of sorts and felt a need to farm in a much larger and diversified manner.

With much begging and cajoling NOT to do so from Lois Marion, he put his family farm up for sale and looked to finding just the right size plot for his needs.

Lois Marion was in a constant state of tears for a long while during this period of time and was extremely frightened for the appearance of a 'gamble' she felt her husband should not take at so young an age. She did have to admit however that so far their time on the farm on Highway 47 had been overall prosperous. They were well on their way to a profitable second income even though there had been hardships.

The terrible life threatening work accident in 1964 had taken its toll on Charles' overall health and his wife's stamina as well. The head injury suffered in January of that year would leave a huge scar over his right eye. His overall determination on his health however was that he would overcome and persevere until he met his goal.

He WOULD assure his success and follow his father's lesson to be totally debt free by the age of 50. In order to accomplish that goal, he HAD to take some risks and he was ready for the challenge.

The problem as Lois Marion saw it however was that she feared they were taking steps backward. She feared the price they might have to pay to move up to success may be too great. She was more conservative and fearful of risks.

In 1969 the chance came to purchase a 320 acre farm touted as one of the highest points in the county on one tract of land. The homestead on the old farm had in place an old wooden framed 3 bedroom, 1 bathroom house which was livable, however a far cry from their present lovely brick abode.

She was horrified when she realized he had all intentions of buying that huge farm and her beloved house on Highway 47 was to be sold.

One especially trying and sad day she sought comfort from her beloved grandmother, Eva Marion, who asked her "Marion…do you LOVE him?"

With tears in her eyes she replied "Yes, Grandmother, more than my own life!"

"Do you think you can stay in that house if he decides to go without you?" Grandmother asked.

Sadly she admitted "Well, if you put it that way, no...no...I guess I absolutely could not do that."

With much love and tenderness, Grandmother Eva Marion counseled. "Then what you have to do is put your mind to making a 'different' life in a 'different' address and between the two of you work toward a family goal."

Eva Marion softly and gently whispered to her firstborn granddaughter "Put your mind to it girl, pray for guidance and trust in the Lord."

With that recommendation, knowing the hardships of her own mother, Lois Annie and now hearing it from her beloved Grandmother's mouth she set her mind and heart to the task at hand.

The new farm on Pinemount in the northwestern part of the county was found to be a beautiful place to behold. One mile deep by one half mile wide, it sat on the most beautiful high spot in the county, complete with yet another huge stand of mature pecan trees. The farm had been mainly hay and cattle producing land and the green fields were extremely inviting. The fact that it also had a pond for fishing and irrigation was a wonderful asset as well!

Charles Henry had experienced many wonderful times over his lifetime when he was most content with an old fashioned cane pole in his hand and fishing for his dinner. If truth be told, fishing in the local ponds and rivers then frying up his catch for his friends and neighbors made for the happiest times during his life.

There were many possibilities for that piece of land; he thought he had died and gone to heaven!

For her part and despite her husband's promise of a bigger and better house one day, she was totally devastated at the prospect.

The family farm sold and he set about moving his family to the little wooden house on the hill of that beautiful 320 acres.

Just before moving to the larger farm and as her husband was nearing his fortieth birthday she decided it was her turn to surprise him and throw a surprise birthday bash. He was forever surprising her with things, some very inexpensive but heart felt and some very expensive as well over the years. He proved to be a very generous and sharing man.

The property was high on the top of a huge hill and once at the top of the homestead, one could see for miles in any given direction. From the county hard road however the roadway took a very sharp turn, effectively blocking a driver's view above until out of that turn.

The young wife set about inviting family, friends, church membership and co-workers, any and all were welcome to come surprise her love on his birthday that December 1970. The plans were made, invitees offered to bring covered dishes and Lois Marion and her daughters made ready for a huge bonfire in the yard of the new homestead.

The wooden house was vacant but the electricity remained for their needs.

His good friend was recruited to drive the farm owner out to the farm on the pretext of viewing his new land. Charles was only too proud to share his new place with his friend. His friend however made excuses and non-important errands before driving out which was beginning to make the new landowner nervous about the time.

(Years later, his friend would comment "Charlie was like a stick of dynamite just waiting for the match by the time we got on our way to the farm!")

Just before dusk, as the car was finally pointed towards the new farm together they joked and laughed their way to the new destination.

As the car exited the very sharp turn on the hard road finally bringing his new farm into view, he shouted "Look, there's a huge fire on my place… Oh my Lord, my farm is on fire!"

His wife had already had a huge bonfire started and his friend knew what was going on so tried to laugh it off. "Charles, don't worry, that CAN'T be your place; let's just get a little closer and I think you'll find it's not even near your farm at all! Let's not jump to conclusions just yet!"

With eyes wide Charles answers "No, I'm SURE that's my place and it looks like there are a bunch of people around a bonfire. My Lord, there's a bunch of kids trespassing on my property! I sure wish I had a phone to call the sheriff and have them kids thrown off" he snarled.

The trip continued with a very nervous and anxious landowner in the passenger's seat. The closer they got to the farm, the madder he became!

His friend counseled "No, don't go off hot-headed and make the situation worse than it might be. It looks like we might be outnumbered anyway! Go easy buddy!"

As they travelled up the long dirt road he began to recognize individuals and wondered *just what right do they have to come out and 'squat' on my land?* The ride was interminable but the closer they came to the home site, the more people he recognized, HIS DAUGHTERS included!

Spewing in anger, he became a raging bull! "What in the world do those kids think they're doing up here…I wonder if their Mama knows where they are!"

The party-goers became aware of the approaching vehicle and made ready to see if it was the honoree or not. "It's Charles…everybody gather together and get ready to sing Happy Birthday to him" his wife excitedly shouted! The revelers surged toward the car just as Charles Henry was ready to charge the crowd!

He had not seen his young wife's face before this time but when she stepped forward and began singing to him he realized they were not trespassers; they were here to CELEBRATE him!

He felt about an inch tall at that moment; he had been mustering up a fight and felt totally justified in so doing! Instead, his love had planned and executed a wonderful surprise birthday party just for him!

(THIS time however, there was no question of his TRUE age; she KNEW since she had already been down that road once before!)

The rest of that evening was spent in wonderful fellowship with family, friends and church members. All present enjoyed the blush of surprise and shock on the face of Charles Henry that night for years to come!

He was famous for pranks and surprises but his young wife had 'sho nuff' pulled a good one on HIM tonight!

The celebration had been a wonderful surprise and left many party-goers with the sweet blush of fellowship and joy.

After the wonderful surprise, however, the day finally came for the family to leave their red brick home. Lois Marion sorrowfully set her mind to making a home in the much smaller and older wooden home. They were now a family of three young teenaged girls with their parents and <u>ONE</u> *stinkin'* bathroom yet again!

She made the most of that little house, heat and all since there was no air conditioning. They had never had an air conditioner even though the times would have allowed. They had always made do with the natural air flow through the stand of those pecan trees and most summers were survivable and most times pleasant if truth be known.

There were many hours spent lounging outdoors in garden chairs shelling peas, shucking corn and pulling peanuts from their vines under the graceful old pecan trees.

She continued baking and decorating cakes and vowed to make the most of what she considered a step backward and a bad situation, however, she determined she would persevere.

The little kitchen was extremely small and old fashioned, opening out to a screened very small back porch. She could not open the refrigerator and oven door at the same time since they knocked together, and left no room in which to maneuver. It was miserably hot while baking those cakes but she tried to keep her temper and do the best she could.

During one of those especially hot days, her husband had an occasion to cook a meal in that tiny, stifling hot kitchen and was drenched with sweat before he finished! The next day he arrived home with a huge window air conditioner to cool the entire house! It was placed in the window of the dining room off the kitchen and cooled the house beautifully.

The one problem it produced however was one could NOT carry on a conversation at the dinner table when the thing was running! Meal times sometimes produced such a cacophony of sounds, the resultant screaming to overcome the din of the a/c totally drained every one present!

All it had taken was one meal in her hot kitchen to make his mind up what needed to be done. He could not force his beautiful wife to continue sweltering in the heat to make extra money.

Farther back on the property stood a smaller wooden house which Charles Henry and Lois Marion had oft-times allowed families in need to move into. It was offered to help needy in hopes to get 'em back on their feet.

There would be many families moving in and out, some paying, some not but over the years the young couple would help others in need where possible.

One such couple was an older African American family from New Jersey who had moved south to be closer to his family. The estate where they had worked had been owned by an older couple and at their demise the estate was sold off, and the cook and chauffeur had been forced to move south. Charles Henry opened his doors to this couple and grew to love both. Dessie was a cook of the highest caliber.

One year for Mother's Day he hired her to cook a most impressive meal with which to surprise Lois Marion. The day was a beautiful day and unbeknown to Charles Henry, she arrived to <u>serve</u> the entire family then returned to her home to be celebrated by her own family. He was highly appreciative and impressed but made sure she could enjoy <u>her</u> Mother's Day as well!

Joe had been a chauffeur and gardener for the family in New Jersey but knew very little about farming on a large scale. The young farmer took him under his wing in an attempt to teach him the farm life.

The older couple was determined not to have a handout. They were proud and honorable people and intended to work for the roof over their heads. They would try any and all things new. In the beginning the proceeds of the farm were not enough to warrant full time pay for his new friends and unfortunately their friends felt they just could not make a living working only part time.

It wasn't long afterwards their beloved Joe and Dessie decided they were not cut out for the Florida farm life and returned home to their New Jersey roots.

The young family was very saddened to lose their friends but respected their choice.

One year Charles Henry had planted a huge stand of tobacco and while still in the little wooden house had loaded the one tobacco barn located adjacent to the home.

All the four girls had been home during this night and at two o'clock in the morning had been awakened by the sound of running footsteps on the screened porch and very loud banging on the front door.

Charles Henry jumped up, hastily pulled his pants over his shorts and ran to the front door to see who in the world would be banging and hollering so loudly at the door.

"Your house is on fire man…can't you see it?" a very loud male voice was heard.

When the residents of the little wooden house looked to the west, all they could see was a huge fireball eating away at the gas cooking barn. It was just about to blow!

The neighbor who had been awake at that time of night happened to look up on the hill to see a ball of fire and possessed the presence of mind to call the Rural Fire Squad. The fire engines had arrived post haste and were able to extinguish the flames before the entire property and trees went up in flames.

Charles Henry's home was saved, his family was safe but he had lost not only a complete day's cooking of that treasured crop, he had also lost the barn and all the cooking burners. It was a devastating loss to the finances! He was fortunate however that his extremely expensive fleet of farming tractors and implements were not close enough to have been damaged at all!

"Take your blessins where you fine em" he counseled.

The loss of that barn would clear the way for a new site on which he would install a brand new mobile home with three bedrooms and one bath (just for the girls). The kitchen of that mobile home would serve for a few years of baking Lois Marion's wonderful cakes and keep them out from under his elbows at mealtime.

The oldest daughter had now returned home (for the second home-coming) so it worked out there was a bedroom for each daughter and now an extra BATHROOM for those girls as well!

He was becoming quite adept at landing on his feet!

The House on the Hill

In the early seventies Charles Henry made good on his promise to build the new brick home for his lady love. Together they found just the right plans and set about building the beautiful new home. It would be much larger than the former home on Highway 47 and most certainly had many more luxuries than their little house on Fifth Street or the little wooden house they began life in on this new farm.

The proper colors of carpet, drapes, wall paper and fixtures were chosen. She would finally have the wonderfully modern huge new kitchen set out just like she wanted. She required a large window for the breakfast room where they could survey the property when at mealtimes. Her kitchen window faced the county road to view visitors arriving by their long dirt driveway to the home.

The three younger daughters had the luxury of picking out just the right decorations for their new rooms and all was going well for the family.

They sold the little wooden house to a young man at Charles Henry's work who hired a moving company to relocate it to his own land. The mobile home was sold and removed from the property as well.

It was around this time the two of them negotiated her retirement from baking all those wonderful cakes. After two decades of baking and decorating many birthday, wedding and all occasion cakes for their community, it was finally time for her to retire. He had promised her the big new house and in turn she had promised him she would give up the baking. It was becoming just too much and required entirely too much standing on her already damaged legs heavily scarred with varicose veins.

By the year 1972, the oldest daughter had met and married her love, Naser, a gentleman from the faraway culture of Iran. They would be married that year and begin their lives together. They moved to a city 50 miles to the southeast in order to allow his continuation of college studies.

The family continued their usual invitations for parties and any occasion to share a meal with any and all who would come. Church picnics were held on the beautiful grounds and many family reunions, wedding rehearsal dinners and any other occasion would be held therein.

Many fish fries were also held and the head of this household was proud to be the one to cook the fish, fries and hush puppies all himself. He many times would invite his mother in law's brothers and sisters for the 'sister and brother' reunion and many times would find him with a gas fired fryer cooking up his treasured mess of fried chicken or fried beef tripe. Lois Marion was always his help-mate with the cooking and together they served many meals over the years.

Eventually he decided each time they invited others to their home; too much work was involved for his wife preparing and cleaning the home for visitors. She accomplished all her housework and chauffeuring duties daily in driving each of the three daughters to their school, church and social activities.

He decided to build a completely separate facility in the place where the old tobacco barn had burned down. It was also the same location where the mobile home had been placed providing the overflow for children in their home and now it would house "Charlie's front porch."

It was a lovely white frame building, large enough to handle over 100 guests including furniture enough to seat many around the beautiful fireplace. There were sofas enough to offer sleeping accommodations for four overnight guests. The building possessed a full bathroom and kitchen which would leave the party facilities separate from the main house.

With a sparkle in his green eyes he teased her "This will let Mama leave her bed unmade and dishes in the sink and nobody will be the wiser!" He understood perfectly well how hard she worked all the years they had been together and wanted his 'bride' to be as pampered as possible! (That is, within reason of course!)

The front and back porches featured two beautiful handmade porch swings built from seconds of water skies harvested from a factory near the famous Cypress Gardens.

He was very proud of these swings and the beautiful varnished wood featured varied colors of gorgeous natural hardwoods. He had instructed the builder to make the swings wide enough to place his iced tea glass held safely beside him while enjoying the glide of the swing. There would be no spilled beverages in these swings, they were beautifully hand-crafted and made to order just for him.

Many comfortable afternoons and early evenings were spent by the family on 'Charlie's Front Porch' and in fact, the very last family snapshot was taken of a very serene Grandmother Eva Marion in this treasured family party facility one day before she passed this life.

One year he decided his bride needed a new ride and decided to surprise her with a brand new car.

All plans were made; he went down to the local Oldsmobile dealership and picked out a beautiful Oldsmobile Ninety Eight with every toy on it possible. It was a beautiful car. He planned just how he was going to surprise her with her new ride.

It was during the fall of the year when the family was again gathering those wonderful pecans and selling them at market. Lois Marion's Aunt Marie always wanted a few pounds of pecans for her wonderful fruit cakes yearly so the nuts were set aside in the garage.

Charles Henry sent his wife to town for an errand he said he couldn't do himself and he and the children planned the big reveal upon her return.

Before she left her home she had left strict instructions with the girls "This bag of pecans is for Aunt Marie. Make sure she gets them when she comes" and assumed her instructions would be followed.

In the meantime Charles Henry had the car delivered to her new home and parked it inside her enclosed garage. He had also made sure clothes were strung up on the clothesline inside the garage, effectively hiding the new car from view within the house.

Arriving home in the farm truck with her task completed, she entered through the back door, never having any inkling her own car was no longer parked within her garage.

She went to the kitchen where the three younger girls were busily putting the meal on the table and hollered to anyone who would listen "Did Aunt Marie get her pecans?" She knew her Aunt had been by but wanted to make sure someone would remember to hand off the treasured nuts.

The three girls looked one to the other and each shrugged! "I didn't give them to her...did you?" to the other. "No, I didn't give them to her either."

By this time Lois Marion was becoming perturbed that her instructions may not have been followed and began toward the utility room and into the garage, Charles Henry in pursuit as well. The entire family went to the garage to see if the bag was still there.

By this time she was becoming angry and Charles Henry just stood there...not saying a word.

She was on the verge of venting her anger when Charles Henry simply said "Mama, is there something different in the garage, Love?"

Surprised she stammered..."Well no...I don't see anything different...is the bag of nuts over there on the other side of my car?" She continued looking to the west side of the garage and never even noticed the new car. She was THAT intent on finding that bag of nuts!

By this time the girls began to snicker to each other and their Daddy was grinning from ear to ear but Lois Marion was totally clueless what her family was laughing about!

Charles Henry walked over to the clothes line and began removing the clothes, opening her line of view to her brand new chariot! "Oh…what in the world have you done Honey…is this for ME?" she hollered.

With a huge grin on his face and his twinkling green eyes alight he affirmed "Yep…it's all for you!"

The automobile was as big as a Sherman Tank and the girls all told her so but she was "proud as punch" her man would pick out such a beautiful and luxurious car for her to drive. She was one happy farmer's wife that day and the farmer was one happy husband to pull off yet another great surprise as well!

One afternoon in the early seventies the couple decided to check on the cow and hog trough located a short distance down the property. They walked hand in hand down the pasture toward the feeding trough with the little cocker spaniel inherited from Daughter #1 who decided to trail along with them.

During those years the farmer had been raising and selling many Black Angus cows and hogs as well. All were within the confines of the portion of land where the trough was located. An old fence stood on only one side of the trough and offered no hindrance to keep the animals from entering.

The little dog, exuberant and joyful in his yapping and running to and fro through the pasture began chasing the herd on every occasion. He was in absolute heaven!

When the couple checked on the trough and looked around, to their horror they realized the little dog was rushing in and out of the cows and stirring up much ire! The cows began rushing the dog as well and it became a cat and mouse game for a little while. All the while, the farmer was hollering for the dog to come to his side.

Of course, the dog was having no part of it; he was having far too much fun!

Unfortunately, when the dog understood the herd was running towards him, he then decided it was time to retreat to his owners' sides for protection, tail tucked between his legs! He was leading the entire stampeding herd directly to THEM!

Charles Henry realized that now the entire herd was moving toward that little black and white yapping terror within their midst. When he realized the presence of the charging herd, his sense of danger quickly arose and he screamed to his wife, "Run, Marion, run like the devil, I'll try to scare them off from here. Just get the heck out of here!"

Lois Marion was totally caught off guard but only heard the words "Run like the devil" from her love. In her haste, she began running towards safety, the little dog now yelping in absolute terror. Apparently she was single minded and with an impaired sense of distance ran toward the only <u>fenced</u> portion of the property!

She struggled to jump over the old fence and with relief stopped on the 'safe side' turning finally to see where her husband was now running!

She wondered, *is he safe? My Lord, here come the cows right after all of us!*

She turned and made like the wind towards the top of the property where she knew the cows could not enter. She prayed her husband was close behind. Once safely over the remaining fence she realized with horror and much embarrassment that indeed he was running from that charging herd but he didn't have a need to jump OVER the fence. He merely ran AROUND it!

The absolute laughter between the couple that day when she took the time to <u>climb</u> the useless fence instead of running <u>around</u> it was a source of great pleasure for years after and still brings comic relief to family gatherings!

The lesson learned that day was when striking out for a walk within the pasture where his herd of cattle grazed, he must make sure that danged dog stayed at the house!

Charles Henry and Lois Marion late seventies

The Middle Years

During the years of 1974 through 1978, Dell Anne and husband, Naser brought a son, Boback and a daughter, Shaida into the family and they were much loved by their Grandparents and aunts.

The years passed quickly; Charles Henry had made many successful choices in his real estate and crops and they were becoming very comfortable financially. Those who had known the humble beginnings of the young couple were proud of their success.

Lois Marion, Lois Annie and all four daughters faithfully raised their voices in the church choir.

When together, the couple <u>still</u> held hands whenever possible and he kept his promise of both a departure kiss and an arrival kiss for his love.

Charles Henry progressed within the Power Company and eventually moved from lineman of the company to district supervisor for three counties towards his retirement years.

As he had promised his bride when she moved from her treasured house on Highway 47, he built the wonderful new home on the hill and she was very proud to host many events in that home as well as the party house.

However, Charles Henry, having added onto their first home and built two more homes over the years had begun to take a real interest in construction. His home had been furnished with many new gadgets for the time and he took great pride in the beauty of his surroundings. Lois Marion had an idea of just what colors she desired and made a very comfortable home for all.

The year of their 25th wedding anniversary, Charles Henry decided he didn't especially like the family/living room of the house on the hill and decided to extend the length of the back of the home farther to the south. The size of the room would be tremendous and would serve as two separate seating areas with a beautiful Italian marble hearth surrounding his beloved fireplace.

He had not installed a fireplace in the house on Highway 47 and had not initially built one in the house on the hill either. However, if he planned to go to the expense of extending the house, there should now be a fireplace installed.

He set about designing the room with multiple windows and a new entrance opening from a covered back porch where he once again installed a lovely porch ski swing. When completed the family would marvel at the beauty of the fireplace in the winters where the huge extended hearth tiles extended far out into the room. With low lighting in the room the fires danced within the fireplace and appeared as millions of diamonds dancing upon the marble tiled shiny surfaces. A lovely mesmerizing show of lights could be enjoyed by the resident occupants.

When the anniversary of their wedding was to be observed he declared there was going to be a formal reception for his love since they had not been able to afford both a formal wedding celebration AND a reception all those years ago.

Their daughters were all grown by now (or at least young teenagers), and Lois Annie was still sharing their lives faithfully and often. Life was good.

The girls all decided they would wear their best 'frocks' and Charles Henry would wear a suit (which usually he only wore on Sunday-go-to-meeting days or funerals but for which he would acquiesce this one day). His usual mode of dress upon arriving home from work was to immediately don his treasured and faded "overhauls" (overalls). Around sun-down he was most-times found sitting either on one of his beloved porch swings with a glass of iced tea or relaxing in his recliner after a hard day of work and farming.

It was a family joke told over the years (but it was actually true) that any time 'Daddy' rattled his glass, the sound of tinkling ice within his glass would bring five women to their feet to refill it. He could be sitting at the dinner table, on his porch swing or in his recliner and the tinkling of that ice would produce the desired affect...ANYTIME!

With this movement however, all his 'girls' would be rewarded with the beautiful twinkling green eyed grin he would flash their way along with his wonderful chuckle!

Lois Marion purchased a lovely gown and made her own 25th anniversary wedding cake which was set up formally in the beautiful dining room. Many guests were received, any and all acquaintances were invited and no one went hungry that day.

Charles Henry's sisters and their families came from down south and helped cook, serve, celebrate then clean up the remnants of the day's celebration.

The couple was thrilled the event was so well attended; it proved to be a wonderful day of fellowship and celebration.

Both secretly wished they could witness those 'nay-sayers' all those years before who were convinced the couple was too young to marry saying "that marriage won't last."

Charles Henry's farming was running full steam ahead as he had concentrated on building a very large herd of Black Angus cows. The day came for delivery of his latest purchase, a livestock hauling truck loaded with ALL heavily pregnant beautiful black cows. It was a family event the day the cows were delivered and all gathered at the field to watch the new bovines arrive.

Of course, one who has ever seen a truck loaded with livestock of any kind knows the delivery also contains a very large and usually pungent load of excrement along with the herd!

The first cows to be led down the chute from the truck of course had 'accidents' on the way down. Even though the chutes were built with criss-crossing pieces of stabilizing boards, each successive cow on its way down the chute would slip and slide on the now mounting piles of excrement!

The vision brought the family to tears of laughter to see huge cows sliding down the slippery chute; a veritable *bovine sliding board!* The anxious eyes of the cows would prove their fear. However, once gaining a firm footing on solid ground began 'feeling their oats' and ran frolicking into their new green fields of home!

It was a sight to behold!

Charles Henry worried about any of his precious cargo losing their calves on the journey but all appeared safe and sound and not one of those new calves was lost that year.

His herd was growing and he was devoted to making sure they stayed healthy until time for market. This investment would be great but he knew the gamble could one day increase his fortune...or break him totally.

He had purchased a huge flatbed farm truck on which he piled the bales of hay and single-handedly fed his cows from the back of his truck each day.

The property was very high and the pastures had a nice roll downward to the county roadway. He knew the exact location where he could safely put the old truck into neutral, rig the steering wheel safely, climb back onto the back of the truck, and allow the truck to continue its downward momentum totally driverless.

Once on the flatbed he would throw off hay bales to the cows within equal distances all the way down the hill. Upon his arrival to the bottom of the hill he would be able to safely climb back into the driver's seat and drive the old truck back to the barn, never missing a beat.

Since the motor was not even running during this chore, he even saved fuel for the truck! Watching this afternoon feeding routine brought much delight to the entire family and proved their Daddy could do ANYTHING! He could have demanded his daughters go out and help but he always focused on their school work and instructed them to "help Mama first." He would make do with what he had.

Of course Lois Marion could drive that huge old truck just as well as he since it would be she who was nominated to pick up the livestock feed while he worked at the Power Company. It was quite a funny sight for their daughters to see this tiny, pretty little woman driving the great big old farm truck loaded with sacks of feed!

The beauty of it was that even after working in the fields, driving tractors, trucks and anything else needing to be done on the farm, Lois Marion could kick off her farm boots and gloves and put on her prettiest set of high heels, earbobs and Sunday hat and appear just as genteel as any of the best of 'em!

Sunday brought out her loveliest frocks, perfectly bejeweled as well!

She had a penchant for matching and colorful jewelry and all dresses would be bedecked with earbobs, necklace and bracelets perfectly coordinated. She had quite a collection of beautiful antique and new jewelry and never tires of anything new and sparkly.

One day after church services, a couple standing with their precocious little daughter were speaking with a friend of Lois Marion's and could not place who she might be. Lois Marion's friend began describing who she was and the little girl with a gleam in her eye spoke out "Oh…I know her…she's the sparkly lady!" She was absolutely right of course and Charles Henry was very proud of his sparkly Bride! (Charles Henry was right "Mama 'sho nuff' do clean up good!")

As the couple grew into their middle years, it became necessary for Charles Henry to watch his health a little more closely and he decided he would begin jogging down the very long dirt driveway to the paper box each morning around 4:30 AM. The long dirt road held some of the most pleasant grass and sand and he marveled at how exhilarating it was to run bare footed down the path each morning. There were no fences in the interior of the pasture and at the end of the road was a very sturdy cattle guard built deep into the earth. This cattle guard was a series of extremely heavy metal bars planted over the opening of his drive just at the main county road but would disallow the cows from entering the roadway. It was a very old method of containing cows but was extremely serviceable.

The thought of having to put a gate over the driveway and opening and closing each time anyone entered or exited the property just was not a pleasant thought; the cattle guard would do the job!

One early, very dark and cool morning he sat on the porch swing, rolled his britches legs up and proceeded to make his way once again down to the paper box. Even though the moon gave very little light and there were no street lights installed on the county road, he knew his way by heart. He knew every little bump in the driveway and didn't feel a need to carry a flashlight.

The morning was cool and crisp and the pleasure of the cool sand and grass between his toes as he jogged brought so much gladness to his heart, he felt on top of the world!

His wonder at his success caused a little prayer upward thanking his maker for showing the way. He thanked God for his life, his family and his love. As he was running farther down the road he heard a strange and unfamiliar sound.

"BPLWWWFF" could only be described as the sound as it sent a chill up his spine.

He just couldn't place the sound.

He could see nothing as it was darker than dark at that moment and could only feel a presence. The feeling made the hairs on the back of his neck stand on end but he didn't stop, he just gathered up his courage and continued on his appointed round. With a nervous glance around him he thought. *No going back now, I'm almost there!*

The sound began coming off from his opposite side now… BPLWWWWFFFFF" came another sound! His curiosity and anticipation was getting the best of him as he wondered out loud "What the devil IS that?"

With his heart in his mouth he continued his run, all the while thinking *this is just getting toooo weird! I don't know what's out here but I'm sure feeling uncomfortable, WHATEVER it is!* (One can only imagine the thoughts running through his head at this time since no moon light was showing him the source of the strange sounds.)

Again he hears BPLWWWWFFFFF then another BPLWWWW FFFFF!

Suddenly he realizes he is completely surrounded by whatever is making that horrible noise! With the very next step he stumbles upon something very large in his path and goes down for the count! His heart is beating wildly as he tries unsuccessfully to right himself and find out what in the world he has gotten into!

All of a sudden the entire country side erupts into a cacophony of blowing sounds, snorting and ungodly screeching! He was 'sho nuff' scared now and most definitely about to GET THE HECK OUT OF HERE!

He didn't know which way to run…should he run to the north…to the south…to the east? It seemed in any given direction, those weird sounds were emanating from everywhere!

With fervent prayer he thought *oh God, let me out of this mess…let me get back to the house!* It was only when he decided to head for the security light on the top of the hill and the safety of his house that his common sense kicked in and told him *wait a minute Charlie…just stay calm, there is a logical explanation for this; just calm down!*

At this moment with an extreme sense of relief he realized his unknowing forced entrance into this huge mass of SOMETHING was in fact his own herd of cattle all peacefully resting right in the middle of his lovely driveway!

HE HAD BEEN THE INTRUDER...NOT HIS COWS!

As he had been getting closer and closer, the cows had been blowing as they many times do in warning of approaching danger. They were all laying down which caused the commotion when they had to hurriedly jump to their feet at the perceived danger of a stranger. They had been just as blinded by the absence of moonlight as he!

The herd was sent helter-skelter across Charles Henry's beautiful pastures in absolute terror!

THAT was a stampede this early moon-less morning and something of legend if truth be told!

When Charles Henry was able to catch his breath and slow his rapid heartbeat down he began to chuckle to himself...*You fool, Charlie, why would you think nothing could be in your way out there anyway? Don't you know them cows go anywhere they want to in your fields? Why in the world would you think you wouldn't need to light your way down here, you idiot? Those cows are as black as night and you can't even see the whites of their eyes!*

By the time he arrived back to the house, he was laughing so hard he couldn't catch his breath! "HRRRRR, HARRRR, HARRRR, HRRRRRUFFF" he hollered.

She had been standing in her night clothes in the kitchen beginning her morning chores and heard his loud laughter all the way from outside. "Shhhhh, Charles, the girls don't need to get up just now. What in the world are you laughing about, Love?" she asked.

Hysterically laughing now, "Well, let me tell you, Marion. I just had the scare of my life out there in the driveway just now."

With concern written on her face she asked "What happened?"

With tears of laughter he said "I heard some real strange sounds and got scared to death when I fell over something huge in the roadway. You won't believe it but I just ran right smack dab into the herd in the middle of the driveway!"

Laughing now but with much concern she asks "Are you okay, did you get hurt?"

Tears of mirth now running down his face he replied "Well, no, I'm not hurt but I'm not sure who was more SCARED....ME or those black COWS!"

The girls awoke that morning to the sounds of their parents' extreme laughter and <u>all</u> would chuckle secretly when imagining their father's fall and his total fright!

The Later Years

Good times and bad were experienced in that house on the hill. When the time arrived he had made his fortune and no longer desired to till the earth Charles Henry sold the largest portion of the property to a farmer from Indiana.

With a laugh and a wink he told his bride "Well, Honey, I think it's time to retire from farming; I think I've had enough now." Her heart soared and she clapped her hands in joy at this news. She had been waiting for this day for way too many years to even count!

She knew this would require the loss of her beautiful house on the hill but she was prepared and knew he would build another just for them.

The chance arose to purchase another 25 acres closer to the county road and he built almost the exact plan from the house on the hill. She was able to decorate it to her liking and he was pleased to offer her yet another beautiful home on twelve and one half acres. The other half he sold to a friend who in turn built a lovely family home there as well.

During the years, the three younger daughters had graduated from high school, attended their respective colleges and chosen their mates.

Charlene married Dave and brought David IV, Charles and Raeghan to the fold.

Kay Sue married her love from college, Gerry and brought Christopher to the family.

Nola Jane and Bob, (the boy next door) married and became a family as well.

The daughters and new husbands made their own lives together, building their new homes and garnering new careers. The three younger girls would move farther away from their parents; Dell Anne, Naser, Bobby and Shaida remained the closest of all the brood for most of those years.

Maude and Nita's children married, had children and made their own respective fortunes.

The years were close, family times were abundant and trips back and forth to 'home' bring pleasant memories of days gone by. The couple, now 'empty nesters' lived in their new home for only a few months when Charles Henry got the urge to build again.

This time he set his sights on a lovely 12 acre plot of land on the banks of the natural lake in their home town where his love had learned to swim all those years ago. She was not so thrilled about moving lakeside since yet again she felt "perfectly comfortable right here."

The words of his father, William Henry, all those long years ago kept returning to him, "Son, you need to own the roof over your head and be totally debt free by the time you are fifty". He had already accomplished that lifelong goal and was proud to say it. His only regret was neither his beloved mother nor father were there to witness his success first-hand.

With the profits from the farm, his farming activities over the years, his real estate transactions and his frugality, he had amassed a great sum of funds and decided "It's time for another change!"

He was still working at his job but had given up the farming altogether (with the exception of the family plots in which he still grew vegetables every year).

The large lake-front property where his bride had learned to swim so many years before was proudly purchased and while showing his bride and her mother the new home-site, Lois Marion was horrified! When they drove to the property, the undergrowth was so thick they couldn't even see the earth. All they could see was the natural pond where he wanted to stock catfish for his fishing pleasure. They could not see the location where he wanted to construct the house and neither his love nor her mother could see his vision.

Both were hesitant to show their true fears but also knew if he was determined…he <u>would</u> build. They both trusted his judgment however, but prayed for success.

In 1982 he began pouring over new house plans and grudgingly Lois Marion took interest yet again since she had already learned when he got something in his mind, there wasn't much to change it! At his insistence, she took the plan book, pouring over each and every plan in that book, studying and figuring the room sizes, locations of closets, door and windows, all that makes up a good house plan. After a few days of religiously and honestly studying the right plan she turned to the dog-eared page in the book in which he had instructed her to make a choice.

With resignation she pointed to the page and said "Honey, if you must build another house, then THIS is the one I would like you to build."

He grinned mischievously and excitedly shouted to her "Well, that's 'sho nuff' a coincidence; that's the one <u>I</u> picked too!" (One could only wonder if in fact this WAS his choice at all. Their lives had been filled with instances of his making her believe things were HIS choices when in fact many times it would be HER desires he followed!)

He would be the planter of ideas, nurturer of the visions and master of devotion to his love. "Happy wife; happy life." he would sometimes jokingly comment to others.

The huge traditional home was built complete with window blinds sealed within each window. With a mischievous grin he would comment "Now Mama won't have to warsh the winders." (Wash the windows...) She would give him the sweetest smile and in her heart would totally agree with the sentiment...joke or not!

The house was built in such a fashion for a view of his beautiful lake from one side of the house and yet another view from his breezeway porch ski swings; this view offering full view of his catfish pond. The pond was his pride and joy where he had planted hundreds of beautiful day lilies at the south end of the shore. The graceful branches draping over the water reflected the beautiful nature of the surroundings and proved extremely peaceful and serene scenery. This lovely pond reflected their love from so many years before, pictures of the young couple standing calf-deep in dark waters are treasures kept within the family. (See Cover photo of Charles Henry's pond with teenagers Charles and Marion standing in the water. Lois Marion's photo as a teenager is to the left of the couple.)

The property would be their lifelong residence for both and would bring many more happy family gatherings, brother and sister catfish dinners for Lois Annie's surviving siblings, an eightieth birthday celebration for Lois Annie, reunions and get-togethers of family and friends.

The grandchildren would anxiously await their next trip to Grandmother's house and all would be happy and safe in the 'house that love built.'

He had a very long deck constructed out into the lake with a large central area that could be used for fishing and steps entering into the water for swimming. He was very concerned about the older 'widder ladies' (widows) in the church membership and would invite anyone who cared to visit their home to fish to their hearts' content. He would even sometimes offer to clean their fish for them.

The loss of his own mother so early in his life made him very tender hearted for the older women and he often would wonder to himself what life would have held for him if his mother and father had survived longer into his own adulthood. He fervently prayed they would be proud.

Wanalee, a lovely lady and widow of one of Charles Henry's very close friends loved to fish and hunt and he would allow her free reign of the fishing dock.

In later years when the rain levels in Florida began to decrease thus causing the water levels of the lake to recede he extended the deck on out another fifty feet into the water to allow their continued fishing in deep waters.

Eventually he decided he wanted a boat so he could take his family and friends out onto the lake for fishing and 'just because' rides around the huge lake. The boat was a ten passenger pontoon boat and many trips were taken in that boat over the years by all.

Lois Marion had a very close cousin, Crockett who married his high school sweetheart, Annie Merle and the two couples were as close as a military career would allow them to be. When Crockett retired from the military and returned to his home town, he purchased a farm in a rural area of the community

One beautiful Saturday late afternoon the couple arrived for a meal on the lake with Charles Henry and Lois Marion. The ladies made a wonderful meal and carried it out to the pontoon where their waiting husbands were anxiously seated. The afternoon was just at dusk and the waters gently slapped against the sides of the pontoon.

Charles Henry maneuvered the boat through a shallow area connecting the smaller body of water to the larger and set for open water. The lake is a very large fresh water lake, one of the cleanest in the State. However the water is very dark with tannic acid. Many fish are in that water as well as alligators, turtles and snakes. The edges of the lake are heavy with ancient Cyprus trees and near the shores beautifully flowered lily pads and natural vegetation offered much beauty.

There were only two areas on the lake where boaters could actually set their boats into the water and one was privately owned, thus keeping large numbers of boats off the pristine waters. The absence of public access to the waters helped keep them as natural and clean as possible.

He owned his own lakeside property which allowed him to park his boat on his own dock and would require no need to find other methods of setting his boat into the lake. His boat remained permanently docked at his back door.

The two couples cruised for a little as he found just the right spot to drift a while as they enjoyed the prepared feast. The evening was just cool enough to be pleasant and the lights danced upon the waters like diamonds.

While they enjoyed their repast someone noticed the sun just on the edge of the horizon to the west and it was showering the world with the most glorious hues imaginable. The western sunset was absolutely magnificent; the beautiful gold rendered God's beautiful pallet of color. Someone turned to the east and realized at the same time as they viewed a beautiful vibrant sunset, the full moon was coming up in the east as well. The waterway upon which the boat traversed projected illuminations of both the west and the east sky and the magnificent gold all at the same time!

For just a few moments the couples enjoyed the most breathtaking visions ever beheld! In the middle of God's beautiful waters they witnessed the glory of truly an *On Golden Pond Moment!*

They spent a lovely evening, none wanting to venture back to land. The gentle rocking of the boat was almost surreal. The joy of the witnessed golden sunset remained gloriously fresh in their memories.

Eventually they knew they needed to return soon so grudgingly began the ride back to the dock and back to their respective lives. Begrudging the hour approaching, Crockett and Annie Merle offered their thanks for a wonderful evening with great fellowship and took leave towards their own home.

Charles Henry and Lois Marion gave thanks, having been blessed to receive such a wondrous vision of Mother Earth and were grateful for all their many blessings.

The two couples would reminisce about that lovely day for years afterwards but none would ever witness the same beautiful miracle again. That treasure was a memory retained deep within all their souls for a lifetime.

(Marion and Charles walking the same aisle of their own wedding on the occasion of their daughter's marriage early eighties)

The Twilight Years

Early in Robert Dale's business career and when he was becoming financially very successful, he purchased a lovely home in Murphreesboro, Tennessee. Charles Henry and Lois Marion desired a visit to his new home so asked daughter #1 to drive there for a few days. They went for only a short visit since Charles Henry's mantra was when visiting others "Don't stay more than 3 days cause houseguests are like fish…after 3 days they begin to stink." (He certainly didn't believe that of visitors to HIS home however; the longer, the better!)

Robert's mother, Juanita was now living in Nashville; the trip would be two-fold; a visit with Juanita and with Robert Dale as well.

A story must be related at this time to explain the beauty and meaning of Charles Henry's next feat of hilarity against his beloved young nephew:

MMMMMMMMAAAAAAAAAAAAAAAAAAAAKKKKKKKK!!!

There came a time in the career of Robert Dale, now known as TheRobertD and his celebrity Andy Andrews that the need arose to travel to 'The Islands' for a film shoot. After their work had been completed they enjoyed a little sight-seeing before heading back to their respective work and home areas. The beauty of the area was enjoyed by all.

In their travels in a public area with much vegetation and tropical foliage they came upon a very large lizard-like reptile sunning itself. It was not an alligator or crocodile and was not a Komodo dragon but something on that order. Whatever its exact species however, it was MUCH larger than lizards we see here in the States. Being ever adventurous and curious, TheRobertD ventured closer and ever closer to study this unusual creature.

The overall appearance of the beast was more formidable and dangerous to all except TheRobertD who felt a need to check this critter out. Ever so carefully he inched closer and closer to the still resting creature; the human so quiet and stealthy he was barely breathing…

With total amazement, curiosity and exhilaration, TheRobertD came as close as he could possibly get to the resting creature without disturbing it.

Unsure if the creature was even living he was so still, TheRobertD slowly and cautiously crouched down to visualize the scaly appearance of this unfamiliar creature. He was, however, prepared to *move like Moody's Goose* if need be!

As he was studying the form of this seemingly docile creature, suddenly with a spontaneous start the creature dramatically and thoroughly sent a serious warning to stay clear!

In an instant, the creature was reared back on its hind legs, fore legs pawing at the air and with the most menacing and scary sound ever heard, sent the message, **STAY AWAY!**

MMMMMMMMMMMAAAAAAAAAAAAAAAA KKKKKK KKKKKKKKKKKKKKKKKKKKK! The creature roared; his wide open mouth showing a distinctly dangerous and menacing set of choppers!

Again he screamed, still reared back on his hind legs, **MAAAAAAA AAAAAAAAKKKKK!**

The human, TheRobertD was so frightened he jumped two feet in the air probably never even having caught traction! His movement was so quick surely he must have flown to safety, never having touched down to earth! He only began breathing again when he arrived at the awaiting vehicle and once removing EVERYONE from his path, parked himself inside safely enclosed within the steel cage of safety! (One imagines his heartbeat could have been heard from a ten foot distance!)

Stories told over the years of this incident have brought tears of laughter and Robert Dale gives the greeting at every possible chance. Of course comedian TheRobertD tells the story best of all and **MMMAAAKKKK** has become somewhat of a trademark for this very successful businessman.

After the first telling of this story during the previously mentioned visit by Charles Henry, Lois Marion and daughter #1, Dell Anne, the occasion arose to use his trademark greeting against nephew Robert Dale in a most appropriate and hilarious method and Charles Henry was primed and ready!

At the time of the visit in question at Robert Dale's new home in Tennessee, his work ethic was such that he accomplished a lot of telephone work late at night and in the wee hours of the mornings. It was the nature of the beast in his line of work since his celebrity's events involved evening music concerts and engagements.

Consequently, at the time of their visit, he was not necessarily an early riser, at least not as early as his Uncle Charles. Around 9:00 AM on that third day of the visit the trio were up and ready to start that ten hour trek back to Northeast Florida. The older couple's time clocks have always been on Florida 'farm time', which means before the sun comes up you need to be ready to go to work. Also, when Charles Henry's feet started 'curling round the perch' it meant he was going to bed with the chickens (or when the sun went down).

Consequently, he was always the first one up in the mornings and the first one into bed at night. For him, the nine o'clock hour meant that half the day was already gone!

The threesome had already had breakfast and Charles Henry had packed his suitcase (or had his wife do it) and were sitting downstairs waiting for Robert Dale to rise and shine.

Charles Henry kept looking at the time. (He never wore a watch but could tell the time of day by the location of the sun.) He knew *that boy* needed to get up so they could leave. He also felt very strongly that when leaving someone's house after they have hosted your stay, you need to at least tell them goodbye in person. You don't just sneak out the door in the early morning hours!

The house was a beautiful rambling two story house with the living room ceiling open to the second floor and all the bedrooms of the home as well. Banisters and railings went completely around the entire second floor and included the entrances to each bedroom. One could stand up above from any one of the bedrooms and view the entire living room down below. It was a very open and beautiful home.

Charles Henry began to fidget and pace around the room, looking up periodically to see when *that boy* would be coming downstairs so he could tell him goodbye. He always had a habit of jingling the change in his pocket as he paced so he was beginning to make some kind of racket as it was. His agitation was increasing by the minute. His time clock was on GO!

Before Lois Marion and their daughter could stop him, Charles Henry stood in the middle of the room DETERMINED to get *that boy* out of bed so they could start the long trip back to Florida.

"MMMMMMMMMAAAAAAAAAAAAAAA AKKKKKKK KKKKK…MMMMAAAKKKKK…MMMMMMMM MMMMMMMMMMMMMAAAAAAAAAAAAAAAAAAA KKKKKKK" he hollered at the top of his lungs!

The sounds reverberated around that huge room and it seemed the rafters were shaking from the din! If there had been a decibel meter handy that morning, surely it would have registered well above the legal limit!

Robert Dale has been blessed with an extremely heavy and bountiful head of hair and every hair is in place at any given time. So bountiful that Charles Henry would tease him about that *pelt*…"don't you think it's time for a haircut son?" might be periodic admonishments over the years.

Welllll…NOT THIS TIME!

He came charging out of the bedroom with every hair standing straight on end as if he had placed one finger into an electrical socket for a good charge!

His eyes were wild as he stumbled from his bedroom and with both hands on the railings to the upper floor screamed at Charles Henry **"HENRY, HAVE YOU LOST YOUR EVERLOVING MIND? YOU SCARED THE PI#$ OUT OF ME!!!"**

The outright laughter began, quickly swelling into a great crescendo…

"HHRRRRRRRRR…HHAAARRRRRR…HHAA RRRRRR" Charles Henry screamed! Lois Marion and daughter were fearful they would have to retrieve Charles Henry from the floor where he was laughing so hysterically. They were both tearful with mirth in their own rights!

By the time all realized what had just occurred, the din of laughter that morning in Murphreesboro, Tennessee surely could have been heard all the way into Nashville!

The trip home from Tennessee was spent in smiling, giggling then outright GUFFAWWWWS all the way back to Florida! Surely Robert Dale will find some way to get back at his beloved Uncle…SOME DAY… SOMEHOW!

Charles Henry had continued on with his job until his fifty seventh year of life, retiring from a managerial position after years of devotion to his company.

Even though the years of work had been at times grueling and many times frustrating when politics were involved, he felt an obligation to his company but more to provide for his family. Decisions made to remain in positions through the years had to be balanced between his need to move ahead and his desire to provide for his girls.

The day of his retirement, his mind was sent back to a simpler place and time when he had been forced to watch his beloved father die an early death near penniless and never owning a home for his family. He mourned his father's loss of a young wife and being forced to raise children all on his own in a very difficult time in history. He mourned his own loss in losing his mother and his father as well.

He had become the Patriarch of his family at the young and tender age of twenty one but had never looked back. His history was just that…*history* and he determined he would make good on his promise to his young bride, to succeed and give his family much more than he had in his early life.

His hard work and determination had paid off and he shared his wealth and lessons freely. He took special interest in his nieces and nephews and had tried to instill in them the lessons of hard work, integrity and sharing. He had always had his eyes on the horizon with hopes of making a brighter future for his family and he was a proud man.

One day while seated at his breakfast table with his love, he became very quiet and pensive.

She asked him "What's wrong, Honey…is there something bothering you?"

With hesitation and tears in his beautiful green eyes, he related a story from so long ago he had never shared with anyone. He had kept the pain within his heart since he was six years old during the illness and subsequent loss of his mother, Ola Dell.

He related the story to her quietly streaming tears down his face even after all those years. He was now in his late fifties and the event still haunted him. "Mama was really sick after Nita was born and Maude and I were at home with her while Daddy was working in the back forty over at the old farm.

Mama started getting really agitated and we didn't know how to help her. She called me over to the bedside and told me to run to the field and get Daddy. She needed him in a hurry" he continued.

Slowly now and with many tears he related "I ran as fast as I could down to the field and had to pass by our neighbor's house. Daddy was working in the back of their farm so I went up to the house and talked to the lady of the house to learn where I could find him.

I told her Mama was calling for Daddy and I needed to fetch him home, it was an emergency" he continued. "The lady told me she was sending her son down to the field to get Daddy and she wanted me to go outside and play with the children until her son and Daddy could come up to the house. Everybody around the community knew Mama was really sick after Nita was born and then she had a stroke and got even worse. I think that lady knew something major was happening and she wanted her son who was bigger than me to hurry as fast as he could to get Daddy so we could go back to our house."

With heavy sorrow he related how his father came upon him playing in the front yard with the children and they both struck out quickly back to their own home.

"Daddy didn't say anything to me while we were hurrying home but when we got to the house Mama had already died. She died without us and I was running as fast as I could to get Daddy for her to talk to. He didn't make it back in time; she was already gone when he got there" he sobbed.

Struggling to maintain his composure now he told his bride "You know, Daddy was so distraught and angry that he turned to me and told me that *he should beat my butt!*"

With many tears falling now he continued "I guess he thought I had been playing when he got up to the house but he didn't even stop to find out; he just jumped all over me like it was my fault my Mama died without him.

"You know, that was the most hurtful thing that ever happened to me in my life and I've never been able to tell anyone till now. It has been in the back of my mind all these years and it just needed to come out!"

She held her husband's hand and soothed his pain as much as she could. They both wept over one painful moment retained in his heart all those years and it broke her heart to see him so distraught. Together they shared each other's pain and held each other until the tears subsided.

The lesson of the retelling of that day however would impact his family that *words spoken in anger can hurt for a lifetime. They can also be impossible to retract.*

The bonding was complete; he knew they had made the right choices in each other all those long years ago. Together they had suffered through hardships but had been totally devoted to each other all those years. They would remain so for the duration of their lives.

He marveled at how fortunate he was to have gotten through all the trials and tribulations of a life with four daughters, now sons-in-law and grandchildren. There had been good times and bad no doubt but he had to give thanks for all he had received. He was still as devoted to his bride as ever before and was grateful for his life.

He was without debt and his bank account was comfortable. He would not, however, be frivolous. His tithes to his home church were generous both financially and in support of the maintenance of the buildings as well. He knew his accumulated finances would need to see the both of them through to the ends of their earthly walk.

Lois Annie had been forced to move into their home on the lake in her twilight years when her health would no longer allow her to live alone in her treasured home. When the house plans had been in the research stage, he had declared there was to be one room especially for his beloved mother-in-law. He knew the day might come when she would need to be cared for in her twilight years and included her in the planning of which room would be hers, how large, how many windows it would contain and how to decorate it.

She always loved him for his caring ways and remembered all the years he had watched out over her as a young man and had helped him in turn in all ways she could as well.

They had been blessed with a very loving relationship over the years, respecting each other immensely.

The day came when she moved in and the room was decorated to her satisfaction. She spent the remaining years of her life with her daughter and treasured son-in-law in 'the house that love built' on the lake. Before her final days on earth her health failed considerably requiring a live-in caretaker. Myrna was a blessing to the entire family when she moved in. She was given her own room and since she was trained in the medical field was able to help Lois Annie with her personal hygiene needs and also helped tremendously in the general care of the home as well. The help was much appreciated by all.

When Lois Annie's days on this earth were completed in 1996, the house was returned to the residence of only Charles Henry and Lois Marion and they yet again felt "empty nesters."

Their lives were rich and full; they devoted much time to their church activities, travelled the world in cruises each enjoying the other in their twilight years.

Charles Henry and Lois Marion with grandson,
Chris in Hawaii early nineties

The church community looked up to them for their generous tithes, devotion to the church family and willingness to help any and all they could. Neither turned down an opportunity to give and Charles Henry served as deacon of the church, building contractor, general laborer, fund raiser, material purchaser and treasurer for many terms over his lifetime. He later would be successful in building the beautiful new 17,000 square foot

Fellowship Hall building at their family church which to this day remains a testament to his devotion.

Marion and Charles cutting the ribbon to the official
Fellowship Hall at their home church

He felt no amount of money was too much to make sure his bride enjoyed her retirement just the same as he. He was mindful of the fact that she did not have a 'day job' to attend each day as he did but she had toiled just as hard and long as he had nonetheless.

Those years were precious and each time the opportunity came for family and friends to visit all enjoyed the times spent together. The couple was famous for calling friends and relatives and requesting a visit "We'll bring vittles" he would say. Long distance trips to Tampa many times would bring a covered dish luncheon in the trunk of his vehicle to his sister Maude and cousins. They would drive the three hour trip down for the day, have their lunch together then drive back home again that afternoon.

Over the years, Robert Dale had threatened his Uncle Charles that he was going to **"jump on your bed"** which would yet again bring a very stern and threatening stare from the Patriarch of the family. *The look* had dissuaded the nephew all his life and so far as the family knows the opportunity had not come to pass. That is, until much later in life at a family event when the daughters were all adults with families of their own and Charles Henry and Lois Marion were in their twilight years.

Robert Dale was now a much sought after business associate with an extremely successful and financially rewarding career.

On one occasion, the family gathered at the wedding of Mary's daughter, Angela where each couple booked a room in the hotel where the reception was to be held. After the reception and before the adults went to their respective rooms, Robert Dale wanted to see "Uncle Charles' room." The group travelled with him to the hotel room where all gathered; daughters, husbands, Lois Marion and Charles Henry. Robert Dale was 'feeling his oats' that night and unknown to all proceeded to accomplish his long threatened feat to **"jump on your bed!"**

Surely he must have felt this must be his pay-back time for the fright suffered in Murfreesboro!

The event happened so fast no one was able to comprehend since everyone thought surely he was joking.

Not so!

All 6'2" of this very professional and successful businessman, perfect business suit, tie and shiny shoes, took a running start and landed right in the middle of Charles Henry's king sized bed where he continued jumping up and down, almost crowning himself with the ceiling!

Initially, the girls and their husbands were so shocked there was no reaction. Very quickly however everyone in the room was howling with laughter except Charles Henry who stood rooted to the floor starring...*the look*...the dreaded *look* from so long ago...no laughter...no spoken word... nothing but **the look**!

Lois Marion's expression was that of a *deer caught in the headlights*, she had no idea what was going to happen next!

After a few jumps, uncontrollable laughter and whoops of joy, he jumped off the bed and sidled past his Uncle who still wore the dreaded **look** on his face. As the beloved nephew decided he had done his promised deed and *still* no reaction from his Uncle, he left the room. His parting words to the group as he sidled out of his Uncle and Aunt's hotel room that night were **"Whooo BOY, I' didn't know whether to scratch my watch or wind my butt!** *The look* **STILL gets to me!"**

HOWLS of laughter erupted as they proceeded to his cousin's rooms where he continued jumping on their beds as well, business suit, shoes and all!

Unknown to all of the family but Lois Marion, however, when their children and Robert Dale left their room, Charles Henry erupted into such a fit of uncontrollable laughter, the couple stayed up half the night reliving and totally savoring the look on Robert Dale's face and the comments upon his departure as he skulked out the doorway!

Charles Henry couldn't even stand up he was so tickled and collapsed onto the bed where the couple giggled like schoolchildren all through the rest of the night!

That evening brought such laughter and the telling and re-telling of the tale left many visitors to their home reeling with laughter at the imagination of the event!

Charles Henry's bank account remained nicely sufficient and he would assure his wife's protection for her remaining earthly walk even if he was not blessed to remain with her. He hoped for many more years together. For his part however, he would make sure she received all he could give her.

One such frivolous expenditure however would be the great pride of his life; the day he surprised his beautiful wife with a new piano.

Lois Marion as a child had wanted to learn to play the piano. In those days of hardship there would be no money or opportunity for the little girl to receive such lessons or even the luxury of owning a piano.

During a time of great hardship for the family due to a strike with the Power Company, Charles Henry felt a need to return to work before the strike ended. His family was the most important of all and he had disagreed with the ideas of his co-workers. He was a man who appreciated his company for all he had accomplished in his career.

A man of great integrity, he voiced his opinion and decision much to the displeasure of others when he stated his intentions. He had very strong opinions about hard work and appreciation for a good day's work for a good day's pay. He was thankful for what he had. His need to take a stand would be repeated in later years but he did not waiver in his beliefs of "right is right."

Those stands for right would cause him great hardship over the years but he stood his ground and prayed for guidance, winning 'right' or not.

During the last days of the strike and when he had returned to work, he gathered enough funds to pay for a beautiful new console piano upon which all his girls could practice their music.

The ages of the three younger daughters were such that Lois Marion enrolled them into a neighborhood piano class in town and remained in town after their school classes long enough for their piano lessons. Each week would find three little girls taking turns at their teacher's piano to learn how to play. The girls all excelled and at the first opportunity, Lois Marion herself decided it was now time for HER to train as well.

She paid for her lessons and all four banged on the piano for years.

After all her children had left home she continued her lessons, fervently practicing every day and Charles Henry enjoyed the sounds of music emanating from the living room. She had been dedicated to learning her music and was thrilled her daughters excelled. It gave her much pride and a great sense of accomplishment when she played for herself.

He determined THIS gift would be a treasure to remember!

One threatening and cloudy day, while she was practicing her music she heard someone ringing the front doorbell. She opened the door to a very large object being wheeled up their walkway from a delivery truck in the driveway.

Lois Marion recognized the young man Hal and his friend wheeling this large object and when he recognized her he said "Well hello, I thought this was the Murphy residence!"

By this time her husband had moved to the front door to find out what was happening. He witnessed a moving van and somewhat angrily said to his wife "Marion, WHAT in the world have you bought NOW?" (It has always been a family joke whenever Mama bought something for herself, Daddy would usually jokingly say "Bride...you don't need that!")

She was totally taken aback replying "Well, nothing Charles, I have no idea what this is! Hal said he thought this was the Murphy residence!"

By now Charles was interested in the goings on and went to speak with the two men who stood with the very large object already removed from the moving van. She stood in the doorway awaiting the outcome of this visit.

Charles looked to the skies and said to Hal "You know, son, it looks like it's about to rain a big one. You'd might better get that thing on the porch before it starts raining. It's coming any minute!"

Hal looked back at the moving van and realized the distance is much farther than the short walk to the porch so decided to take up the offer of the homeowner and put his package inside before the very threatening skies released their fury. The men inched toward the porch when Charles changed his mind and told them "You know on second thought, bring that thing on inside; it sometimes rains inside that porch too. We'd better be safe than sorry. Besides, my wife here just might want to test that thing out if you wouldn't mind."

Lois Marion listened to the conversations between the men and decided to just stay out of the whole thing; *let him take care of it* she thought to herself. Throughout their lifetimes and with his wit, for many years she might have been just plain gullible! For so long her husband had joked and teased and she just sometimes let his humor roll right off her back!

This time was no exception; she had no clue!

They rolled that package which she realized was a very large brand new piano into the hallway and began moving toward the location of her prized console piano.

Hal looked at the niche in the living room where her much smaller piano sat and asked Charles Henry "Do you think we can move your smaller piano to the hallway and move this bigger one into its place for the time being?"

Charles Henry just shrugged and said "yeah, that's okay, go ahead."

She was beginning to get a little perturbed at their seeming nonchalance in moving her treasured piano out of its home to put someone else's in its place. She normally let her husband do much of the deciding but this decision just might be way too much!

"No, now wait a minute, we don't need to be moving my piano around at all. Let's just put this one over here and it should be okay" she offered.

Her beloved husband, realizing this joke may have gone on long enough, put his arm around her shoulders and with a hug said "Honey, this is YOUR brand new Disclavier. I just wanted to surprise you!" He had researched completely on his own and found a player piano which used computer diskettes to record her music!

Clapping her hands and giggling like a school girl she replied "Oh Charles...this is MINE?"

"Yes Bride, I just knew you would be happy with something like this. Now we can have our girls come home and make beautiful music and we can listen to their recordings any time we want!"

With a joy not felt in a long time she screamed "Charles, what in the world have you done this time? I am absolutely thrilled to have one of these!"

He reached out for her and said, "Yes, Love, I've been figuring to do something for you for a long time and I just thought you might like one of these new computerized piano things!"

She lovingly hugged him and said "You have made me a happy woman today. I never even dreamed I would have one of these all my own!" With that she allowed her old treasured little piano to go back to the music store with the two young delivery men and proceeded to read all the instructions on the brand new contraption.

She played all the pre-recorded songs that came with the instrument and between them and her daughters made many, many more recordings in the following years. Many wonderful hours have been spent over the years sitting at the bench of that beautiful instrument and she would take nothing for the experience of the day he played the trick on her!

He, of course, being the master story teller he was could spin the experience into quite a story which was likewise enjoyed by many friends and family members over the years. The story remains a sweet memory to all.

In 1999 the couple celebrated fifty years of marriage with a huge feast at their home church complete with a catered meal for over 350 people held in the beautiful Fellowship Hall he had been honored to build. The day was much enjoyed by all. Their now grown daughters sang a few old hymns for them and the pictures taken that day show a lively family.

Kay Sue, Charlene, Lois Marion, Charles Henry, Nola Jane and Dell Anne on the couple's fiftieth wedding celebration

Sunset

There came a time in late 2007 where Charles Henry's health began to deteriorate and he suffered problems related to high blood pressure and heart issues. He had been treated for these problems over the years but now was beginning to experience periodic intestinal problems as well.

The time arrived that the doctors felt it necessary to prescribe a blood thinner which severely limited certain foods from his diet and caused many trips to have his blood quality checked on a regular basis. He began to lose his strength but for a man well into his seventies it was a supposed fact of life. They worried but maintained vigilance as much as possible.

During one such bout of problems Lois Marion had gone to a business meeting out of state with daughter, Kay Sue.

His health declined seriously enough to require Dell Anne to take her father to the specialist sixty miles from home. By the time they arrived, he was in serious pain and required intestinal surgery. The surgery was very long and tedious and his health deteriorated greatly.

During his recuperation his strength completely left his body and at one point he was forced to be on a ventilator. The family was greatly concerned and had never seen their Patriarch totally helpless nor speechless. The ventilator prevented his speech and unfortunately he spent Thanksgiving, his seventy seventh birthday, Christmas Day, New Year's Day and his wedding anniversary in a hospital facility of some sort or other.

Over the course of the next year he would move from one facility to another with various rehabilitation centers in between. It was a very sad time for everyone, however, his bride Lois Marion was at his bedside virtually every day during those times of illness.

She no longer felt comfortable driving herself to out of town locations so one of her daughters or sons-in-law would drive her the sixty miles to his bedside, stay with them all day then drive her back home again that evening. This continued 24/7 until she was able to bring him back home again. There were good days and bad during this time and she worried for her love and wasn't ready to give him up just yet.

On December 8, 2007 a letter was received from his nephew who so long ago had been born into the family and had been Dell Anne's adopted baby brother, Robert Dale.

The letter came from a man who had gone on to succeed in his chosen field with much success and offers much inspiration to others. Robert Dale has been a Manager to a very popular inspirational speaker and author over thirty years and together they have amassed an amazing following and fortune. He is an author in his own right as well.

The letter as written on that day from Robert Dale, a loving nephew follows:

December 8, 2007

Dear Uncle Charles:

First of all—HAPPY BIRTHDAY!!!!!!!!! Second, let me say that I've had the MOST wonderful week simply thinking about you and the many ways you've influenced my life!

I must say that getting this chance to share my gratitude is an honor and an outstanding debt I consider long overdue. When my beautiful young mother found herself raising a new baby on her own, her husband off in the Service, she knocked on the door where she knew love lived—that of her older brother. Indeed, you and Aunt Marion opened your home and your hearts without hesitation. For years, you cared for us, loved us and poured yourself into a little boy that wasn't your own—in the midst of raising your own family. During those years the foundations of love and family, my sense of self and my connection to God all were laid in large part, with your able hands.

So much of the "good stuff" in my life started with you. Especially during summers in Junior High—I remember Sundays at church, looking up at the towering ceilings, hearing the music and letting my heart splash joyfully in the awe as I caught wonderful glimpses of God. You could have stayed home on Sundays—could have lived your life much differently—but you didn't. I thank-you for that.

I've watched you live your life with my eyes wide open and my ears peeled. I often think of you when I hear the saying: *Speak the gospel always, and only when necessary, use words.* The sound of your life speaks louder than a dozen sermons. You are a rare man indeed.

Continued . . .

December 8, 2007
Page Two

I have gone on to achieve things in my life I never dreamed possible. Looking back, I can say my greatest joy has been helping others succeed—encouraging them—something you also inspired in me.

You gave me the gift of hard work, one of the most priceless gifts a man can pass on to a boy. I'll never forget the summer I spent with you working on the tobacco farm. The early mornings, the blisters, the searing heat and the satisfaction of collapsing into bed at the end of a hard day's work, is a feeling that continues to bless my journey today.

I closed my eyes today and could hear you laughing your infectious laugh that we all love so much. I could also smell Aunt Marion's cakes baking, their heavenly sweet aroma dancing through the house and wrapping itself around me. I couldn't have dreamed up better memories. Thank-you, Uncle Charles.

Will Rogers once said: *We can't all be heroes, because somebody has to sit on the curb and applaud them when they go by.* Today, it's a joy to sit on the curb and applaud you—a hero whose legacy of integrity, laughter and love will echo through future generations.

Happy Birthday Uncle Charles and THANK-YOU for being a hero to the little boy and a role model to the man. I can only hope my life reflects even a portion of the man you have shown yourself to be.

With gratitude and admiration ~

Love,

Robert D. Smith

P.S. - If I were there — I'd be jumping on your bed! ☺

Letter from Robert Dale Smith, [TheRobertD] on
the occasion of Charles Henry's 77th birthday

The letter written by Robert Dale to his Uncle Charles was greatly appreciated by Charles Henry's entire family and is a favored memento of his love, admiration and respect for a man who gave so much of himself. His love of his Aunt Marion is well documented as well.

Through the following months, Charles Henry's health would improve then relapse and his strength became less and less. Treasured times were spent in 'the house that love built' by the lake and Lois Marion remained his constant companion.

His hospitalizations became more frequent and on Christmas of 2008 the entire family gathered in his family room and exchanged gifts with one another.

Shaida, the oldest Granddaughter had made a beautiful movie of her Grandparent's lives together. No one knew she had been building this beautiful tribute to her Grandmother and Granddaddy and when honored with the copies, of course, all had to watch. During the movie, he sometimes dozed off during the 22 minutes of the telling of their life story. However, when Shaida kissed her Grandfather on the cheek he told her "You got it right, Grand-daughter...you got it right!"

That was the most treasured thank you she could ever have received!

Both of her Grandparents appreciated her time and efforts in telling of their lives and love together.

On January 9, 2009, Dell Anne, Naser, Shaida and Peter, her husband, took a special anniversary meal to the couple and celebrated sixty years of marriage.

To all those nay-sayers from so many years ago who said "It won't last"... This is proof that it DID!

Charles Henry rallied that day, even so far as to walk by himself to his love's car, seat himself in the passenger's seat to show all he was strong enough to go to the market. It was his plan for all his children and grandchildren to gather together for a special meal in honor of their sixtieth wedding anniversary on Saturday, January 17, 2009.

He so looked forward to that day.

On the evening of January 15, 2009 his oxygen level began deteriorating and the hospice doctor declared he should go to the Hospice Facility. He agreed he would go but would walk on his own two feet to the awaiting vehicle in which he would take the ride. He and his beloved bride walked hand in hand once more.

Once there he lay down on the hospital bed and began having problems breathing. The nursing staff gave him medication to ease his symptoms and help him sleep.

He slept soundly well into Friday, January 16, 2009.

Lois Marion and Kay Sue visited him on Friday afternoon when he was rousing.

He opened his beautiful green eyes and gave each one of them a sweet, sweet smile. They were highly excited since it appeared he was finally getting rest.

Those two smiles would be his last…

Nursing staff advised the two to go home and rest, come back in the morning. "We'll call you if there's a change. Let's just let him rest now." Mother and daughter left, each resting very little but each also hoping the next time they saw him, he would be alert and ready to tease once again.

The next morning while Lois Marion and Kay Sue were arriving at the Hospice Facility, the call came that his time was near. As they ran into his room, Lois Marion rushed to his bedside and placed her cheek on his and said "I'm here Daddy, I'm here!"

Cheek to cheek with his lady love, he took his last earthly breath, sixty years and eight days from the day he said "I do"

He waited for his bride; he would not leave this world without his love by his side…

Sweet Sorrow

I am Dell Anne, the eldest daughter of these two loving individuals and relate the following events on the passing of our Patriarch, Charles Henry Hines.

Saturday, January 17, 2009 was to be the day Charles Henry celebrated with all his children and grandchildren around his table once again in honor of a sixty year life with his love, Lois Marion.

Unfortunately that day would be the end of his life at 9:45 AM. The celebration meal would not be taken with our beloved father.

The morning of January 18, 2009, Mama and I were alone in 'the house that love built' on the lake and neither of us were able to sleep the previous night.

It was the first night spent in that house with the knowledge that her love, Charles Henry would never again walk the halls of this beautiful home.

I was in the living room seated in Daddy's favorite recliner and spent most of the night crying and staring at the moving objects on the television.

At 4:05 AM on Sunday morning, January 18, 2009, Mama stumbled to the living room and stood in front of me.

She said only one word "Thirty…"

I asked her "Mama, what did you say? Thirty; what do you mean?"

With a very serene expression on her face she replied "I heard your Daddy's voice and he said simply THIRTY. I have no idea what it means but I was not sleeping, I was not dreaming. I HEARD YOUR DADDY'S VOICE!"

I was fearful she was losing touch with reality so did not question her further on what she was so adamant she heard.

We talked a little but neither of us could sleep. The house was so quiet. We knew there would be a 10:00 AM meeting at the funeral home for final arrangements.

The time arrived for all to gather at the funeral home, we went through all the motions and knew Daddy's wish was for a simple service…nothing grand.

The family had been told of Mama's hearing Daddy's voice and the word "thirty" but no one had any inkling of the meaning. Everyone walked around the room trying to pick out just the right casket and no one could make a decision; so overwhelmed were we. We made yet another trip around all the displays and remained unable to choose or learn the meaning of "thirty."

Kay Sue had been escorting Mama around the room and put her arm around Mama's shoulder. Both turned to the display right in front of them...

Kay Sue cried out "Oh, Mama, here it is...this is what Daddy meant... this casket is $2995."

Everyone even though deep in sadness had to grin a little.

With further emphasis, my little sister, Kay Sue the clown, said to all "You know, Daddy always knew you HATED fractions...he rounded it off for you...THIRTY!"

Tears flowed as well as laughter since it was something Daddy absolutely would have done. Such a joker; even in a time like this he would not have wanted any one of us so deep in sadness. He always told us there was another place, another time and he looked forward to his final rest.

We KNEW our father had been given final passage; and even though we missed him already we were proud and comforted he had finally been rewarded for a life well-lived.

The fact of the matter is that the casket before which my Mama stood WAS the only display in the room near the 'Thirty' price point and it was exactly the style he would have chosen! Understated but sturdy, nothing elaborate or showy for him; a simple man of the earth...

The next task was to choose the verse for the printed service brochure.

We were all so numbed with grief nothing we read from those choices seemed to fit our father. There were numerous verses but Kay Sue's husband, Gerry, said "let's turn to number thirty and see if that might fit. It's worth a try at any rate."

It was perfect; the verse was exactly as our Daddy would have said to us.

I'M FREE – I'm following the path God laid for me, I took his hand when I heard him call, I turned my back and left it all.

We knew immediately it would prove to be the perfect choice.

The evening of visitation for family and friends to pay their last respects came on Monday evening, January 19, 2009 and was very well attended.

Kay Sue, Gerry, Nola Jane and Bob made a beautiful display as a tribute to our father's life.

The display contained baskets of fruits, vegetables and peanuts overflowing; the bounty of Mother Earth, a tobacco crate and hand plow represented the hard work he accomplished in building his life with his love. His hard hat and climbing hooks represented his career with the power company that kept his family fed all those years and finally lovely, lovely flowers, his offering to his childhood love.

Funeral display for Charles Henry Hines 1/19/09

Robert Dale brought his mother, Juanita from Nashville and everyone gathered in Charles Henry and Lois Marion's 'house that love built.' The house was full, many family members and friends from far away states attended and the general feeling was not one of a morose nature. In fact, many jokes related had originated from our Daddy; tears were shed both in sorrow but also in joy for all the love, fun and laughter he brought us.

A friend of Nola Jane's, Linda, came in support of her best friend and would later marvel at the love in the house that evening. She commented it was one of the most joyous bereavements she had ever witnessed.

Charles Henry and Lois Marion had a Jamaican doctor neighbor and over the period of time they lived on the lake made friends with the younger couple.

On the evening of the visitation, the doctor neighbor and his lady arrived to offer their condolences, leaving their car running in the driveway. They recognized the fact many people were in attendance and only wanted to offer condolences to Mama and leave. The Doctor graciously wrote a generous check to donate to our father's favorite organization, his life-long church fellowship. She was honored to receive his gift and offered a seat for them to visit for a while.

Even in her bereavement she would be the gracious hostess.

From the outpouring of love from family, friends, church members and townspeople, the food brought to the house was overflowing and there was plenty to feed all.

Mama graciously invited the couple to partake a meal with us.

At first they were reluctant but she persuaded them to share with us.

A phone call came in and Mama hushed the crowd gathering in the house. It was our 94 year old life-long church pastor calling to pray with our family. The room hushed, every head bowed and our Mama listened to the beautiful prayer offered to the heavens for our father's final flight home.

The moment was cherished and all proceeded to partake of the lovely offerings of food from the community.

The doctor was seated in the breakfast room enjoying his meal when the story came up about how Charlie could only shake his ice cubes in his glass and five women would jump up to fill his glass. He laughed at the story as did everyone in the room.

As he did so, unconsciously *he shook his empty tea glass and at the exact moment, I arrived with a complete beverage refill!*

IT WORKED!

The look on the doctor's face at that moment was one of sheer amazement and wonder and remains a wonderful, light and funny coincidence. The laughter in the house that evening was infectious!

The couple so enjoyed their stay with our family that evening, they completely forgot to turn off the engine to their car. It sat running for over an hour in the driveway, totally abandoned!

The next day was January 20, 2009 and it was time to say a final goodbye.

We traveled to the funeral home, a beautiful service was given and there was standing room only in the funeral home. Mama did not want to remember her love's final repose in front of their home church's altar where they had married all those years before so chose the final celebration to be in the local funeral home.

Charles Henry's older sister Maude attended even though her health was very fragile. Her children and grandchildren took time from their busy lives to celebrate their Patriarch's life and we were greatly honored.

During the singing of his favorite song *Whispering Hope* all four of his daughters, Charlene, Kay Sue, Nola Jane and I sang harmony along with Ken, the choir director.

We were sitting in different sections of the audience but all four of us felt the calling to harmonize for our Daddy just one more time. There had been no pre-arranged plans…we just felt the call and all four responded.

My good friends, Carol and Sherry from my work commented later they were "looking for the backup singers!"

We laid our sweet Daddy to rest for eternity and as the family gathered around his gravesite and all the beautiful flowers were laid over the earth, my wonderful husband, Naser, took five roses and handed one to each of us, first our beautiful Mama, Lois Marion, then Nola Jane, Kay Sue, Charlene and finally me for each of us to place over our father's heart. It was a beautiful act of reverence and I will always be grateful for his simple act of kindness.

Our father, Charles Henry Hines may be gone from our earthly presence but he follows our lives, our loves and sends his blessings every day.

His devotion remains forever and his spirit is always within our midst…

Lois Marion: A Celebration to Remember

October of 2009 brought the eightieth birthday of Charles Henry's bride, Lois Marion. Since his leaving this earth in January she couldn't imagine anything that could cheer her sorrows. Her tears had been her constant companion the entire year and her four daughters thought she needed something to remember.

Over the years we have experienced many "sister slumber parties" with our mother. A different place was chosen each year for a birthday celebration. We have celebrated in Little Rock, Arkansas, Twinsburg, Ohio, Phoenix, Arizona and many other lovely locations including our parents' home on the lake. All have anticipated and enjoyed the yearly get-togethers.

Robert Dale had remembered these celebrations over the years and asked me if he could "crash your party this year."

My reply in turn was "sure, if you HOST the event!"

"You're on", he screamed.

We decided this year his beautiful castle on the mountain in Franklin, Tennessee with its MANY bedrooms and living space would be the perfect location. (His home exceeds most five-star hotels if truth be known.)

He set about inviting his two sisters, Lisa Gail and Sandy and I set about inviting Maude's two daughters, Barbara and Mary. Nola Jane, Kay Sue and Juanita would be there to celebrate as well. Aunt Maude's health however, would not allow her to join in the celebration and our sister Charlene unfortunately was unable to attend that year.

The event included all the family 'sisters' and Robert Dale as the only male to witness the goings on. He had no problems hosting "the ladies" as his professional blog would soon relate.

The day came for the group to travel to Franklin, Tennessee; all flew from a different part of the United States to converge on his hospitality and he was totally "READY." (At least that was his story at the very least!)

The parties were met at the airport with a van large enough to carry all the passengers in one vehicle; his Office Manager acted as chauffeur and tour guide and together they proceeded to "the castle."

Upon our arrival at Robert Dale's home, his beautiful breakfast room was entirely covered in birthday streamers, a five foot balloon birthday cake on the huge table and balloons were tied EVERYWHERE. The room is floor to ceiling (2 stories) with windows looking out onto the top of the exclusive mountain property it sits upon and offers the most beautiful views of nature imaginable.

He had ordered a special chocolate and strawberry concoction large enough to feed an army. Since Robert Dale's special memories include his Aunt's beautiful wedding and decorated cakes, he was especially adamant the decoration of her eightieth birthday cake needed to be magnificent and tasty as well.

We were treated to four huge crock pots of different recipes of soups, catered sandwiches, snacks, drinks, anything he could think of to treat the weary travelers.

A wonderful meal was enjoyed by all, Lois Marion was honored with the singing of the birthday song, everyone ate enough for at least two days then were shown to their respective rooms. We were then told to rest up because "Itineraries are coming for the next three days."

Mama and I were in the King room with on-suite guest bath and when retiring for an afternoon rest, she turned to me and remarked "Well, I sure didn't expect THAT!" Her eyes were sparkling and the tears she shed that afternoon were not of sorrow…but those of absolute joy and honor!

When the 5:00 PM deadline came, all invitees were dressed and excited to see just what Robert Dale had in store. All knew of his hospitality and sense of fun but none knew to what extent he would travel.

The first day's Itinerary was introduced with only vague descriptions of what the evening would hold. It was spent in a lovely restaurant for dinner then back home again…nothing too tiring.

Our Itineraries brought much excitement however when the group was treated to shopping in downtown Brentwood. We enjoyed the day then our host instructed all to sit back and enjoy Nashville; we're on our way to *The Grand Ole Opry Hotel!*

ALL "the ladies" were ready, willing and able to shop to their heart's content! The trip to the museum proved very nostalgic and enjoyable as well.

The hotel enjoys an absolutely beautiful and trendy restaurant within the midst of a breathtaking lobby. The property contains much lush landscaping, a winding river throughout and many sights and sounds to thrill the senses!

Many beautiful sights were pointed out, including rides to view 'celebrity homes;' many adjacent to Robert's own home. The views that fall were spectacular and the guests were treated to another meal out at night fall.

The group attended *The Grand Ole Opry* and Lois Marion especially loved the old songs and the retreat back to times gone by. (The return home brought yet again an opportunity to partake of the birthday 'leftovers and MUCH laughter and story telling!)

The day was wonderful and at evening's end he warned all to make sure and sleep tight because tomorrow would hold a special event.

On Saturday, the Itinerary was completely full starting very early and warned all to "bring your walking shoes because there's going to be LOTS of walking today.

Again all piled into the van and we were on our way; still only small hints about where we were going.

Finally the group was chauffeured into a lovely shopping mall parking lot far away from the crowd where an absolutely beautiful custom coach was idling.

No one expected anything was amiss until Robert Dale stood and hollered "Alright ladies, everybody get your butts out of the van...we are going to take a little trip!"

The group witnessed the idling coach, all black and shiny and perfectly luxurious but as far as they knew, they would only be walking to the adjacent shopping mall.

Not so..."The ladies" were ushered into the extremely comfortable and luxurious custom coach with panoramic viewing windows and custom furniture. The coach held nine sleeping berths, a complete sitting area with wide screen TV in the front for business meetings and a second beautiful meeting room with yet another wide screen TV in the rear. The bathroom was as luxurious as any high end home.

The entire weekend event was 'blogged' by TheRobertD and the humorous clips of text relating the events he tweeted kept many people laughing and wondering what "the ladies" were up to next!

The chauffeured coach took us for a cruise around downtown Nashville then on to Kentucky for an afternoon and evening at *Patty's 1800 Settlement* where an entire original Kentucky settlement has been turned into a series of shops, a photography studio, a wedding chapel, restaurants, museum and a beautiful walking tour throughout the area.

Everyone plundered each and every shop, antique shop, museum, wedding chapel, petting zoo and any establishment through that little settlement until the appointed 6:00 PM dinner setting.

Robert Dale had made reservations for the entire group to partake of a wonderful birthday celebration meal in honor of his eighty year old Aunt Marion...Mama!

The buildings were already decorated for Christmas and were some of the most spectacular ever witnessed. Christmas trees were hung upside down from the rafters of the rooms and each room held a different color and theme of dramatic baubles and lights. The group was placed in the peacock room with a most magnificent Christmas tree decorated entirely with exotic feathers.

The views were mesmerizing! This particular establishment seems to be an exceptionally well visited location for the locals and many out of town visitors as well.

We were seated in the middle of a beautiful room with at least twenty other smaller tables arranged around the walls. Each table was filled with happy diners and the room was extremely lively.

Robert Dale's mantra is *"dessert first... there's SURE to be room!"*

Everyone ordered dessert FIRST as he demanded and proceeded to loudly share the birthday greeting with everyone in the room! (He makes his presence known wherever he goes!)

He led a Happy Birthday song which brought the entire room to sing along as well!

Lois Marion, our Mama, sat in the middle of that huge table, in that lovely room and enjoyed the moment like she had never enjoyed before! When the song completed, everyone in the room clapped and shouted birthday greetings and she was so excited she didn't think she could complete her meal. Other diners in the room asked how old she was and most could not believe how beautiful she was at eighty years old!

She was in her element and we were proud for her!

She did eat her meal however, and the evening was drawn out just as long as possible, her tiny little black eyes sparkling with joy and honor...

When the evening was drawing to a close and all had partaken of the wondrous meal, we *rolled* back into the luxurious coach and were driven the hour and a half back to Franklin and back to the castle; home...

The last day with Robert Dale brought a lovely morning breakfast in the beautiful castle and he had ordered beautiful coffee sets for every attendee of that birthday celebration. Four coffee cups with matching spoons built into the handles and each had the date in honor of Lois Marion engraved on them and were given to each person in attendance.

We were taken downstairs into his massive office and warehouse and made gift baskets of all the books he had produced with instructions to his staff to pack a special box to include the coffee set in each one. He wanted to make sure they got shipped back to each person's correct address. He didn't want anyone having to carry a box of "goodies" in their laps on the planes travelling back home.

Each attendee sadly took their leave and went their separate ways from the airport, dreaming of the previous three day experience. Mama and I flew out together; all others went their separate ways since their home locations were different from the others.

The experience that weekend is one of the most treasured and special of celebrations and is highly appreciated by the daughters of Lois Marion and Charles Henry in honor of our mother.

Robert Dale will never fully comprehend what honor and love he gave his Aunt Lois Marion, our Mama in those three days and I send my special heartfelt thank you for his efforts.

EPILOGUE – A Love Letter from Heaven

Tuesday January 24, 2012 - 12:30 PM

Today I called Mama just to say hello. She was preparing to visit Aunt Doris in the Rehabilitation Hospital. Her Aunt's general emotional outlook is not very positive at the moment and she desperately wants to go to her own home.

Our Mama is now our family's Matriarch and wants to help out in any way possible. She has dearly loved her Aunt Doris her entire lifetime.

Mama has also been dealing with the extremely serious illness her cousin is suffering at the moment and from all accounts, his earthly walk seems nearly complete.

Mama and Daddy were both instrumental in helping this younger cousin, Crockett and his fiancé, Annie Merle marry all those many years ago and have remained very close to each other over the years. The illnesses of both her Aunt and Cousin have been weighing heavily on Mama of late; she dearly misses Charles Henry, our father, and is very sad.

During the course of our conversation Mama related an incident that happened this morning when she decided on a whim to drive Daddy's Bravada up to the mailbox. She had not driven his car in some weeks and no one other than my husband, Naser had been in the locked car in months.

She knew the doors remained locked at all times.

As she entered the car she noticed a sales receipt on the passenger seat and worried Naser had yet again put gasoline into her car when she wasn't looking. My husband, her oldest son-in-law, is famous for filling her car up with gasoline, oil or whatever is needed. Whenever we visit he always fires up the cars and checks for fluid levels.

She said when she picked up the receipt to see just what he had done she was amazed to see the receipt was not a NEW receipt; it was actually dated May 18, 1985, was extremely faded and hard to read, but was for a purchased item from a shop in their home town in northeast Florida.

She knew this receipt had not been in the location on the passenger front seat and asked me if I had seen it since I last drove the car after Daddy left our earthly presence.

My response was absolutely there WAS NO receipt on that seat at any time before and if it was, many riders would have had to sit on it over the course of time since we lost our Daddy in 2009. We were both amazed at where it could have come from.

After Daddy's passing it has been many times I myself have entered this car and looked through each and every compartment, nook and cranny to see just what Daddy had been carrying in his ride all those years ago.

The car is a 1996 Bravada and all the original papers were there, as well as some papers from church activities and various other mementoes contained therein. The pocket change from the last time he drove the car remains as well as a cigar presented by an acquaintance from a long ago birth of a son.

All those treasures, chewing gum and any other things in the car have been lovingly replaced back to their original locations. We drive this car with many fond memories of its former owner and when I drive it, I can still smell and feel my father's earthly presence within the vehicle. It holds great memories for me and brings me comfort. He named this beloved car *Mr. Green* and we have all followed suit in the naming of our own vehicles over the years.

The miracle of the receipt's presence however is not just in finding it after all this time but what the actual purchase is that compels me to note its presence. The receipt is that of the purchase of a part for Mama's Snapper lawn mower bagger which has caused such wondrous laughter and joy to our family regarding our parents' relationship over the years.

I would like to share a story told by my Daddy, Charles Henry:

The 'DON'T GIVE A DURN HAT'

"I bought Mama a real nice riding lawn mower, Snapper is the brand and it's a riding lawn mower so Mama can cut the grass all by herself" he said.

With a chuckle and a wink he continued "You know, sometimes Pa don't get the grass mowed as soon as Mama likes so now she won't have to wait for the old man anymore; she can cut the grass all by herself!"

To that assertion Mama just grinned. She was much determined to keep her new home a show place.

Daddy had gone to all the trouble to plant the multitude of day lilies, azaleas, camellias, citrus trees and all sorts of flowering shrubs and bushes to decorate their house on the lake. He was a proud land owner and wanted the place to be beautiful as well. However, the cutting of the grass was sometimes the very last thing left to do and she felt it needed to be done more frequently than he. We all knew HIS domain was on his trusty John Deere field tractor and that machine had no place on the grounds of their new home. That machine was relegated to the fields.

Mama had stated she didn't particularly like the idea of grass clippings being left in the various lanes and whirls left over from cutting the swatch in her travels but she also knew she would not be able to rake all of them up since the property was much too large to manually do the massive job.

She decided she needed one of those "new-fangled leaf baggers." She wanted her yard to be manicured.

Purring and rubbing her love's arm she asked "Daddy, why don't we look into gettin one of those parts to go on my new riding lawn mower?"

With a loud guffaw he replied "What in the world do you want to do that for, Bride?"

"That's just not necessary and besides you won't be able to empty those big bags out by yourself anyway. Just let the grass clippings rot and make mulch in the grass won't you?"

With a decided note of finality which was NOT lost on Mama he said "No, I don't think you need one of those, just keep on cutting the way you are and the yard will look just fine."

His answer sent her anger soaring which made her more determined to get that bagger one way or another. (One might have seen her mind conjuring up little angry retorts. *I'm a grown woman; I don't have to wait for his approval!)* However, she would not state so out loud. It was not normally her nature to show much anger to him; her manner was normally meek, mild and ladylike.

For the next few weeks she didn't say anything to Daddy about that piece of equipment but her manner left no doubt she was NOT a happy camper in his answer. Quietly she stormed, *how dare he tell me I can't have that part when I'm the one doing the work?*

The summer passed, fall came and went then spring was beginning in that year of 1985. Sometime around May, during the time when the new grass needed to be trimmed, Daddy was able to see the grass was coming in pretty well this year and it looked very healthy as a matter of fact.

Mama had stewed for some time on his absolute determination not to purchase that bagger and took the opportunity to buy it herself <u>with no approval from Daddy</u>. She brought that piece of equipment home and asked Daddy to install it onto her lawn mower.

He was not overly happy she had gone ahead and purchased the equipment and yet again asserted his belief it would not work for their application. "Mama, that thing just won't work like you expect it to, Love!" Nonetheless, he installed it to prove his point.

Mama was very proud of the bagger and decided that very day she was going to have to put it to use. She went inside and changed into her yard clothes, placed a little hat on her head (which was something of a small miracle in itself since she normally had every hair in place at all times) and proceeded outside to start her mowing.

On the first pass through the yard she saw how thoroughly it picked up the grass clippings and on each and every pass over the yard she knew it was picking up much debris but was very proud she was cleaning up the yard so nicely. She was proud of her work and quietly determined, *I'll show him how beautifully I can keep our yard manicured and we won't need to hire a gardener. I can do it myself and I'm certainly not afraid of hard work!*

The day may come they would no longer be able to do the work themselves but for now she would save the money and do it herself.

As she came closer and closer to the new house she began to feel sand and debris brushing up onto the back of her neck and pulled that little hat closer and closer down over her ears. She continued cutting just as hard as she could.

Daddy was sitting on the breezeway in his favorite swing watching her every move but being on notice if she needed his help. He secretly vowed, *if she needs my help, I'll come running as fast as I can to help her. But for now, I'm just going to sit here and watch her work!*

She could see from her vantage point each time she passed his location he was sitting there with a huge grin on his face and she would catch him chuckling at times. However, she was determined to show him she made a good decision on that bagger regardless of what his thoughts were on the subject.

Grinning to herself she thought, *he'll be laughing out the other side of his mouth in a while!*

Each pass became more dusty and dirty than the last and pretty soon she was stirring up the dirt in the yard just like the 'Tasmanian Devil' we used to watch on the Bugs Bunny Cartoons. In it, the creature would be engulfed within his own little tornado of dirt and debris. It was only when he stopped could you see an actual creature there; otherwise, only the tornado was visible and constantly moving.

That vision could describe our Mama on her little riding lawn mower on that day.

She was feeling the magnitude of the dust, dirt and debris deposited down her shirt collar that day and it definitely was NOT comfortable!

Each turn of that mower would make her more and more angry! To further add insult to injury, every glance back at the swing where Daddy sat grinning only made her anger mount higher with each pass around the yard!

Each pass however, would also bring that little hat further and further down over her ears and neck until it was stretched to its limits.

It was with this vision of the Tasmanian Devil that our Mama suddenly stopped the riding lawn mower in the driveway, jumped off the seat, turned off the ignition and swore "I'll NEVER use that thing again…! It's not even cleaning up the leaves; it's just throwing sand EVERYWHERE but mostly on ME!" she angrily stormed.

To this comment, of course, Daddy in his infinite wisdom and joking manner told her "Well, that bagger ain't so much built for picking up leaves over dirt, Baby Doll; it needs grass to keep the sand off you."

With a wink and a grin he said "Where you're cutting is too much dirt and not enough grass".

She just stood and glared, completely covered in sand and dirt!

"Looks like you may be finished for a while right now, what would you like me to do with it?" he offered. (Of course at this point she did not much appreciate <u>any</u> jokes he might come up with; anything he said at this point only made to further stir the pot of ire she was presently cooking.)

Mama's eyes grew very large and she began to fume to herself. *I just can't stand it when he teases like that, he's such a know-it-all! I DO know a little something sometimes! It's just a shame in this case, durn it, he's right! I hate to admit it but there is NO grass here at all; that's why I'm WEARING so much of that stinkin dirt!*

Daddy patiently waited on his swing that day for her reply and when she gave it, he almost fell off the swing in surprise!

"I DON'T GIVE A DURN!" she bellowed.

At this point she threw that filthy little hat down onto the driveway, stomped over to the back door and proceeded inside to clean up! SHE WAS <u>DONE</u> WITH THAT BAGGER!

Daddy could tell what his little joking comment had done to his 'Baby Doll' so elected not to further stir the pot too much but allowed her to go on into the house without further ado, water, sand, dirt, sticks and all covering her from head to toe.

She marched straight into the bathroom where she stripped down and washed acres of dirt, sand and debris out of her clothing, hair and body. SHE WAS COVERED FROM HEAD TO TOE!

She viewed herself in the bathroom mirror and realized she could only see the whites of her own eyes and had complete rings of dirt around eyes, nose and mouth as well. She resembled a little raccoon and appeared to have been wallowing in the mire with the pigs! She was absolutely horrified! *How far have I stooped this time? I was certainly not lady-like in my reaction to Daddy but I just couldn't help it…he made me just soooo mad!*

She took a long time that afternoon cleaning the filth to make her person presentable to her love; all the while trying to find the right thing to say or do to try to smooth over her anger.

She needed to let her husband know she knew he had been right all along. *How do you do that when you have let him see you make such a fool of yourself?* She felt about one inch tall that day. At the completion of this cleansing she retrieved a snack from the kitchen for herself and Daddy and went to sit beside him on their swing.

She said "You know Daddy, I didn't realize I was kicking up so durn much sand and dirt all over the place. I guess you were right, as usual" she demurred "and please forgive me for my temper tantrum."

Daddy, in his jolly and joking manner said "Well, Bride, I just figured when you put your 'DON'T GIVE A DURN hat' on, I wasn't going to persuade you to stop anyway. I just let you go your merry way and wear all the sand you wanted" he grinned "But I knowed you'd back off sooner or later" he said with a hearty laugh.

To this end, both enjoyed a hearty laugh at Mama's expense and she bore up quite well once she received his forgiveness.

However, the memory remained for both regarding what tools may be needed in the future. They also realized the fact that both points of view should be kept in mind when purchasing same.

Days later after the incident, Daddy sat close to his love and handed her a handful of bills.

With much surprise and curiosity she said "Honey, what's this for?"

He began somberly "Well, I knew you didn't want anything further to do with that stinkin bagger so I washed it out real good and returned it to the store where you bought it! You go use this money on whatever else you want to spend it on!"

She kissed her love and thanked her lucky stars for such kindness but knew he would tell and retell his story for years to come. She would need to prepare...

He did tell this tale over many years and each time she would bring that 'DON'T GIVE A DURN hat' out, he would relate the joy of that story all over again to whomever would listen. The story brought much laughter and joy in our family and continues the joy of his life with all of us, although we all know they are now memories of our beloved Daddy that can never be replaced. These memories are treasured by all.

On this present day in 2012, with the belief the receipt was NOT in that location in the car previously I assert my belief this may well have been yet another sign of a love and devotion between two people that transcended a marriage over sixty years and eight days.

169

There is no reason a receipt from 1985 would be in the car when he didn't even buy this car until 1996...

I can find no other explanation of how it came to be in that location, or why it showed in clear view on the passenger seat only to our Mama but I can only imagine in my own mind that a divine intervention had occurred to tell our Mama that our Daddy was watching out over her.

It is within this realm both she and I are taking this incident and it gives us both much pleasure. At the time of its initial presence, however, it caused such a flood of emotion from Mama she could only be alone and cry until her tears dried.

After all, we all know tears are cleansing to the soul and she has been *much cleansed* these last years since he left our presence. In the retelling of the wonder of the incident, this story came into both of our minds and brought such joyous memories to both of us; it can only be described as a gift.

At this writing I am so blessed and thankful I was able to share with Mama this joy in remembrance and for whatever reason the receipt was in this spot at this time, I will forever consider the recovery as a sweet message and reminder of the joy, humor and love Daddy gave us and the gifts left for our Mama.

The fact the receipt of this wondrous gift happened on yet another Tuesday, the same as all those years before when both had treasured receipt of their respective love letters, made this occasion even more special. Tuesday, January 24, 2012 would bring yet another 'treasure' to our mother...the knowledge that her love was still devoted to her!

This was truly a special message sent from a heart; or was it actually yet another love letter from her lifelong love...?

Saturday Morning, November 17, 2012

Mama and I are travelling to Amelia Island, Florida to visit the scene of a certain beauty contest wherein my mother, Lois Marion was contestant number 25 on March 14, 1948.

I am revisiting a certain locale to renew my sweet Mama's memory of days gone. This, my second book on my family relates the story of devotion of my parents, Charles Henry and Lois Marion Hines. My words and ability to put them into print has only come late in my life but I have felt a calling to relate their lives for those descendants following our earthly paths.

I was fortunate to have located the new owners of the gardens in which the beauty contest took place all those years ago in 1948 and have been gathering historical data and documents.

Cathy and Dennis Harbin of Amelia Island are the new owners of the property from so long ago and have divided the land into beautiful home sites on which new homes are being built in the 1940s period of the original gardens. Many of the original camellia, azalea and rose bushes remain in this lovely tract of land near the water's edge.

Dennis has been concentrating on unearthing the many plants and concrete borders of the original gardens abandoned by the owner, Mr. GG Gerbing around the year 1950. Soon thereafter, Mr. Gerbing sold the nursery and garden to an associate, Ralph May while Mr. Gerbing pursued other ventures in Fernandina.

The land became over grown by the normal processes associated with years of neglect in a Florida wilderness.

In the early nineties, the land was purchased by the family of the Edwards Pie Company out of Atlanta, Georgia. Cathy Edwards Harbin and husband, Dennis Harbin are the present owners of the approximately 7 acres of the original gardens.

They are the developers of 6 home sites with a 3 acre common area which is to be restored to the original Gardens as designed by Mr. Gerbing.

The architectural guidelines of the homes and gardens are being carefully managed by Dennis and Cathy where their home *Camellia Cottage* is the model.

Cathy and Dennis graciously invited my mother and me to visit and we were greatly excited to make their acquaintances.

We arrived at the lovely cottage and gardens by 10:15 AM and were warmly greeted by this wonderful couple who were anxious to see what treasures Mama retained from her event so long ago in 1948.

She had kept the original pamphlets from the contest, photos, and autographs of dignitaries including Mr. Gerbing who sponsored the contest. We were excited to find the original tag worn to show her as contestant #25 in the beauty contest.

The Archives of American Gardens at the Smithsonian Institution contain visual records of the history of Gerbing's Gardens. Included in the documentation are images of Gerbing's Gardens on the occasion of the beauty contest of 1947. Apparently Cathy and Dennis had no documentation on the 1948 event.

Mama had them all…

The Harbin's possess beautifully framed and protected mementos of events, tracts of property, aerial photos and published documentation on each and every wall in the lovely cottage. It was a joy to witness the historical treasures therein.

Mama had hand-created beautiful embroidered and delicate greeting cards as a hostess gift and I had baked and decorated my own peanut butter cake for lunch. They had graciously and lovingly prepared a lovely lunch for our visit.

A wonderful meal was enjoyed, the conversation lasted well into the afternoon and we travelled down through the gardens and onto the waterfront property.

I grudgingly decided we had infringed upon their privacy long enough and we left their lovely home around 4:30 in the afternoon. We both could have visited with them for hours longer but didn't want to outstay our welcome. Both my Mother and I highly treasure their hospitality and warm friendship.

I had arranged a surprise for Mama in our hotel stay and we travelled to the Ritz-Carlton of Amelia Island, Florida where we were greeted with a lovely Happy 83rd Birthday hand dipped chocolate strawberry concoction made especially for her in our room. Cathy and Dennis had arranged for our lovely room and unbeknown to me the birthday surprise as well.

I took Mama to the original restaurant where she enjoyed the before-pageant banquet in 1948 which remains a well-attended family bar and grill directly on the beach.

We arrived at Sliders Bar and Grill on the beach and were promptly seated.

A large group of bikers arrived complete with leather, *Harley Hawgs*, bandanas, beards and long hair. We obviously stuck out like two sore thumbs;

Mama with her fancy black suit, her sparklies and both of us with our obviously white hairs proved we were definitely out of place!

A table of 8 was seated right next to us and we began to notice the common theme of their jackets and medals. They were obvious Vietnam Veterans and the name of their club was Nam Knights. They were very rowdy and loud with much camaraderie but didn't seem to mind two old ladies within their midst. By the time we left our meal, there were at least another 40 to 50 more of their band of brothers to arrive.

We enjoyed our meal, gave up our booth and quietly left their presence.

The meal was pleasant but she could not conjure up memories of the location other than it was on the waterfront.

Our next trip was to drive downtown to see the lovely lights decorating the shops on the walking avenue. It was 57 degrees and the wind was quite strong so we opted not to shop, besides which, the evening was quickly disappearing.

We drove back to the hotel, strolling through the gift shops in the Ritz Carlton for a little while, soaking up the luxury and opulence of that gorgeous hotel. The decorations and furnishings in the hotel are magnificent, the chandeliers were extremely beautiful and we just drooled over EVERYTHING!

We entered one of the gift shops and struck up a conversation with a lovely young lady working in the shop and made another new friend. She was familiar with our hometown and had experienced a very lovely visit while stranded with a car problem there some years back so had a somewhat soft spot for our town already.

When asked why we were there, I told her it was Mama's 83rd birthday and we were revisiting a time gone by. She was very interested in the Gardens and in fact had some of the memorabilia herself so knew where we had been visiting in the afternoon. During the time we were in the shop, her working partner came in for her shift and a group of about eight customers arrived at the same time. We decided to let the ladies run their shop; we quietly waved a farewell and left the store.

A few moments later as we were about to enter the elevator we heard someone running up to us and realized it was the young lady, Donna, from the hotel gift shop. She wanted Mama's name and what room we were in. We gave her the information and thanked her for a lovely conversation, her new acquaintance, then returned to our room.

An hour later we received a call from the front desk asking could they bring up a gift basket. We could not imagine what this could be but told the bellman yes, we would accept it. When he arrived, the gift basket was a beautiful gift bag with a lovely hand written note to Mama saying how much she enjoyed meeting her, congratulating her on 83 years and on the trip down memory lane.

Inside that gift bag was a very beautiful Ritz Carlton trademarked air diffuser with the hotel's own patented scent. It was a LOVELY and much appreciated gesture on the part of a stranger.

Mama was on cloud nine!

We retired for the night about 10:30 that evening. For the first time in years I was able to sleep continuously an entire night, only awakening at 6:38 AM expecting her to be 'bright eyed and bushy tailed.'

Turning to my beautiful Mama I asked "Mama, did you sleep well?"

With brightness in her eyes I had not witnessed in a while she responded "I didn't catch a wink all night long!"

Alarmed I asked "Mama, was the bed uncomfortable; were you too cold, too warm, were you scared or did you hurt---what in the world was the problem?"

Her answer was a simple and sweet "I just couldn't turn off my brain! I have had a most wonderful day! I kept going over and over and over in my mind all those years ago, the time I spent with your daddy, the day we have had, the new friends we have made and all the wonderful things that have happened to me!"

I took that honest answer as a blessing my efforts and research had given my mother truly a wonderful day!

We enjoyed the scenery in the lovely hotel, stopping to witness a bakery staff constructing a pirate ship made entirely of gingerbread in the lobby. The aroma of the baked gingerbread was mesmerizing. The mast was topped by the glorious lobby chandelier and we would have loved to stay to see the finished product, however, it was not due to be completed until after our departure.

We left the hotel and went back to the gardens for one last look, Mama turning and reliving her experience in the location with the sweetest smile on her face. I took movies and pictures of her traverse down the imaginary runway some 64 years later.

On the way back to her home we stopped in for a brunch in a very lively family restaurant which was quite full as we arrived. Regardless of the number of patrons in the restaurant that day, we were seated very quickly nonetheless.

While waiting for our meal to arrive Mama became quite pensive and mentioned to me "You know, I would just love for your daddy to be here to witness this with me...I miss him so much!"

I could only agree "Me too, Mama!"

I could see she was getting a little misty and I pointed to the chain around her neck. I gently told her "Mama, touch your neck...there..."

She had a bewildered look on her face until she felt the chain around her neck.

My husband and I had given her a beautiful gold chain on which to hang her favored *sparklies.*

She then remembered she was wearing my father's wedding band on that golden chain and the sweet memories overtook the both of us.

With tears in my own eyes, I said "Mama, he DID come with you!"

Very gently she spoke "You know Daddy had it right; he used to say to me we've had a great life, haven't we, Love?"

The sweetness of her smile and the tears we quietly shared together over the blessing of the meal that day will remain in my mind and heart the rest of my life.

Our newfound friendship with Cathy and Dennis Harbin and Donna at the Ritz Carlton Hotel in Amelia Island, Florida made my Mama extremely proud and happy.

I was privileged to offer just one little trip and experience that truly made my sweet Mama happy!

I am truly a blessed daughter indeed!

Dell Anne Hines Afzal
11/18/2012

Lois Marion, *Mama*, 65 years later.
"What a life and experience!"

(Photography courtesy Granddaughter #1, Shaida Afzal Ehlert)

This publication is given in love and honor to both of my parents and will be placed in an honored resting place along with all the beautiful love letters our father wrote to our mother all those wondrous years ago.

They are truly treasures of the highest caliber...
Devotion

I am so grateful they were found in Grandmother's attic after so many years of loss; they are truly Treasures Found.

Dell Anne Hines Afzal